MINI FARMING

A Beginner's Guide to Profiting from Crops, Vegetables and Livestock

By Luke Smith

MINI FARMING

© Copyright 2020 - All rights reserved.

The content contained within this book may not be reproduced, duplicated or transmitted without direct written permission from the author or the publisher.

Under no circumstances will any blame or legal responsibility be held against the publisher, or author, for any damages, reparation, or monetary loss due to the information contained within this book. Either directly or indirectly.

Legal Notice:

This book is copyright protected. This book is only for personal use. You cannot amend, distribute, sell, use, quote or paraphrase any part, or the content within this book, without the consent of the author or publisher.

Disclaimer Notice:

Please note the information contained within this document is for educational and entertainment purposes only. All effort has been executed to present accurate, up to date, and reliable, complete information. No warranties of any kind are declared or implied. Readers acknowledge that the author is not engaging in the rendering of legal, financial, medical or professional advice. The content within this book has been derived from various sources. Please consult a licensed professional before attempting any techniques outlined in this book.

MINI FARMING

By reading this document, the reader agrees that under no circumstances is the author responsible for any losses, direct or indirect, which are incurred as a result of the use of information contained within this document, including, but not limited to, — errors, omissions, or inaccuracies.

MINI FARMING

Table of Contents

Introduction V

Chapter One - Why Mini Farming? 1

Chapter Two - Crop Farming 20

Chapter Three - Profitable Vegetables To Grow 64

Chapter Four - Raising Specialty Livestock For Profit 86

Chapter Five - How To Profit From Mini Farming 110

Chapter Six - Pest Prevention And Maintenance Control .. 125

Final Words 133

INTRODUCTION

There is a misconception in popular opinion that farming refers to large scale operations while gardening is the light version of farming. Gardening, in this sense, is seen as almost entirely providing food for the gardener, often at the expense of a money and time investment. The home gardener is able to supplement their diet and save money on vegetables that they would otherwise have bought, but it isn't considered a profitable venture. If you want to make a profit, then you need to get into farming, but that requires a lot of starting capital to purchase land for the crops, machinery, and labor to work them, as well as legal documentation. A gardener might be able to sell a couple of heads of lettuce at the farmer's market without a problem, but a large scale farming operation requires the farmer to jump through a lot of hoops.

One of the reasons this particular misconception is so potent is the economics behind it. If you try to set up a small farm by following the practices that the industry uses today, then you are going to find yourself breaking even at best. Unfortunately, the odds are stacked against this, and it is much more likely that you will lose money on the endeavor. The problem with turning a profit on a smaller venture in this way is the fact that the techniques used by the agricultural industry are designed for large scale operations. The economics of scale allows for much larger numbers during the production process since the yield of the harvest will be large enough to make up for them. With a small farm, this is just not possible.

But purchasing a large farm isn't viable for 99% of the population. We don't have the resources to invest in buying more land and setting up enough crops to turn a profit. So, it would seem, farming should be left to the professionals and us small-scale growers should stick to our little gardens.

But, thankfully, that isn't true. It is one perspective that seems to jump out from the information available to us, but it isn't the only one. To use a popular metaphor, this perspective sees the glass as half-empty. However, the problem isn't that small-scale farmers can't make a profit. The problem is that small-scale farmers can't make a profit using the techniques and methods of larger-scale farms. This glass-half-full perspective points us towards a new approach, one that *can* profit us: Mini-farming.

Mini-farming uses techniques to compress space and cost to allow farmers more control over their crops or livestock. It is a small-scale approach to farming, but one that is able to net a profit because it doesn't waste time or money on techniques that are outside of its budget. What's even cooler is the amount of variety that mini-farming offers the farmer. Yes, we might set up a crop in a fashion reminiscent of traditional farming, but we could also use hydroponics, raised garden beds, or even simply use containers for our plants. A mini-farm might be grown in your backyard, or it might be grown inside your house. The number of options available is quite high, and when we turn to these techniques, we find that the whole enterprise is much more profitable.

In this book, we're going to cover mini-farming from top to bottom so that you can get started with your own productive and profitable agricultural enterprise. In chapter one, we'll look at the benefits of mini-farming so you can assess whether it is right for you or not. Chapter two will move into crop farming to cover topics like monocropping, crop rotation, raised crops, hydroponic crops, and more. Chapter three continues this discussion by turning to the profitable vegetables that make up those crops. Chapter four will move away from crops to discuss specialty livestock such as goats, cattle, chickens, and bees. We'll have a single goal throughout all these conversations, which is to provide you with the knowledge you need to start a mini-farm that will earn some money. To that end, chapter five looks specifically at profits to see how that money is earned through selling. Finally, we'll close out with a discussion about preventing pests from ruining our farms, and how we can best maintain a high standard of excellence in our venture.

If you have ever wanted to take your gardening skills to the next level and earn money with them, then what are you waiting for? Stop studying the large operations outside of your budget and start mini-farming to maximize your investment and make money.

CHAPTER ONE

WHY MINI FARMING?

We've already touched briefly on several of the reasons why you might want to start using mini-farming techniques. In this chapter, we'll go into each of these (and more) in greater depth. It should be noted beforehand that these reasons don't exist in a vacuum, but rather they interact with and affect each other in a fluid way. This means that we should consider these reasons as building on each other to create a dialogue that encapsulates the subject as a whole. This approach is necessary, as we can't separate these reasons from each other when we put mini-farming into practice. In some ways, that could be seen as a negative. If there was a particular reason that you disagreed with, you can't exactly step away from it or avoid it. However, I'm sure you'll consider each of the following points as benefits rather than limitations.

MINI FARMING

Mini-Farming Requires Less Capital

Farming can be an extremely expensive undertaking. If you approach farming without a concern for the money involved, then it won't be long before you see how much more expensive it is than you imagined. Sure, you're just growing plants in the ground or taking care of livestock, but these create tons of expenses. Some are clear and easy to spot. Others are hidden, only to reveal themselves when you suddenly need to invest more money into the enterprise. This can absolutely devastate your bank account if you aren't careful. A consideration of the costs involved can help to illustrate this.

To begin with, you are going to need seeds. The larger the crop, the more seeds you'll need. Seeds need to be planted in soil, but not just any soil works; it needs to be healthy and nutrient-rich. The crops need to be tilled, and then planted. They'll need to be watered and fertilized. These are all costs you'll need to sink into the farm. You'll also need to pay for the land you are growing on. If you are raising livestock, then you need to purchase food and water for them. They'll need some shelter from the harsher weather conditions. They need to be looked after, kept in good health, and tended to on a daily basis. This can eat up time, or it can eat up money if you've hired an employee to help you. Small amounts of livestock typically don't cause many problems, but the more you are raising, the more likely you are to encounter zoning laws and other issues that need to be resolved beforehand. Of course, legal issues tend to cost a pretty penny themselves. Plus, we haven't even considered the effort or money it takes to keep everything clean and in working condition. And this isn't even bringing in hidden costs such as transportation or taxes.

It can be very, very expensive to start a farm. What's even worse is the fact that most people who are looking to start one are going to need to start small. Just as most businesses need to start small and take time to grow, so does a farm. The end goal might be to become the largest agricultural farm in your local area or even your country, but this takes time to build. When you're starting, if you approach the farm the way you would one of these bigger ones, then you are going to lose a lot of money.

But mini-farming techniques aim to reduce the amount of capital needed to get started. They focus on creating smaller, but more profitable farms. To approach a new farm from the perspective of a large-scale operation will only lead to frustration. These farms are already large enough to be able to afford the steep costs. Their size alone gives them confidence in their ability to turn a profit. But if you are just beginning, then you won't know how much money you'll make with each harvest. Instead of starting large and investing lots of initial capital into the venture, starting with a mini-farming approach will benefit you. You keep the costs low while you go through the process of bringing your first few crops to harvest and getting marketplace data to make profit projections with confidence.

Even if you are aiming to be the biggest, starting with a mini-farm is undoubtedly the way to go. You'll be able to make back your investment and can consider the experience as a hands-on education in the business of farming.

Mini-Farming Requires Less Space

When you look at those larger farms, it can be truly impressive the way they sometimes stretch on for miles at a time. Walking through all of the fields of one of these large-scale farms can easily take up half your day.

However, while there is certainly something very powerful about traversing a farm of this size, it can also be a depressing experience if you are looking to start your own. It would be wonderful if you could have a farm of that size straight out of the gate, but the cost would be colossal. If you always needed that much space in order to start a farm, then nobody ever would. Most of us understand that this is unrealistic to begin with, and so we start at a much smaller scale, but this, in and of itself, is not actually mini-farming.

If you've ever talked with new farmers about how they are beginning, you might have discovered a disappointing idea that seems to reoccur. A lot of new farmers think they need to replicate the planting practices of their colleagues who have larger areas. Yes, they have much less space, and so it is done at a smaller scale, but they still design their fields after the pattern of those larger ones. This isn't necessarily the worst idea in the world; you can still grow some lovely vegetable crops this way. But it is like trying to raise a horse inside your house. Sure, it might fit through the door, but you aren't really using the space available to the best of your ability. For our purposes, this approach is equivalent to traditional farming, but just at a reduced size. It captures one element of mini-farming (the mini part), but it still relies on techniques and approaches designed for larger farms. It is technically using less space, but it isn't using the space in a way that produces benefits from the smaller size. It doesn't turn a potential weakness into a strength.

Mini-farming can be done in various ways and in very different locations, both in size and in environment. Let's say you plant a crop in the backyard, directly into the ground. For simplicity's sake, we will pretend the crop's dimensions are one square foot. This crop takes up that full square foot, and nothing else can be done with this space. If you plant following traditional guidelines, you will only have two rows with two plants each, at best. This space could be used much better. If we tossed out the traditional approach, then we could use what it is called intensive gardening. In this method, plants are grown much closer together. This reduces the amount of space needed, and in doing so, it reduces the amount of care (watering, fertilizing) that needs to be done. We could implement this technique directly in the ground, but it benefits from using a raised garden bed, which brings up another way we can save space. One of the cool things about raised garden beds is that you can design them to have multiple levels. When grown in the ground directly, you have a one square foot crop. If you used a raised garden bed design that had multiple levels, then that same square foot could allow you to raise three times as many plants in the same space.

Reducing the amount of space your crops take up reduces the amount of money spent on soil and fertilizer. It allows you to more easily tend to your crops, as they're packed tightly together instead of spread out. It also allows you to make a higher income because you can earn more money per square foot. So, by using mini farming techniques, you not only reduce the amount of money that you are spending on your farm, but you are also increasing the amount it is earning you. This is an impressive double-whammy that makes mini-farming an attractive prospect.

Mini-Farming is More Productive

To say that mini-farming is more productive is not the same as saying it is more efficient. For that particular reason, you will need to keep reading. Productive here is used to mean that mini-farms produce a larger harvest than traditional farming does. This might seem a little confusing. After all, if it produces more, then why aren't these techniques being more widely used? The answer to this is surprisingly simple. Larger farms have been in operation for much longer, having started their business prior to the scientific revolution that is the mini-farming movement. The older the farm, the more likely it is that old-fashioned farming techniques are being used. Rather than fall into the trap of tradition, we can implement these techniques to achieve massive yields.

When it comes to the gardening component of mini-farming, there is plenty of research to show that intensive gardening practices achieves more abundant results. Likewise, there is also a lot of research that has been done on the use of raised bed gardens. Both of these methods have proven to be more effective than traditional approaches, and this improvement becomes exponential when you practice intensive gardening in raised beds.

This productivity comes at a cost, however. While the yields are bigger, intensive gardening has been shown to have a detrimental effect on the environment. Because of how closely spaced plants are, this approach requires more fertilizer per square foot. Now, to be clear, it requires less fertilizer overall because it is done on a smaller scale, but the amount of fertilizer in any one section is more. To return to our one square foot garden, we would need to fertilize the four plants in the traditional approach, but we could be fertilizing five to ten plants when grown intensively. The problem with this is that it allows for more fertilizer to run off and potentially damage the environment by getting into the water or causing the pH levels of the nearby soil to spike. Neither of these is very positive, and they may be enough to put some farmers off mini-farming.

But if you are careful in the way you design your farm, this won't be a problem. The biggest issue is the possible damage that comes at the cost of productivity, but we've already identified one way of reducing this. If we design raised garden beds that are at least a foot tall, then we can use a solid bottom to prevent too much fertilizer from getting out. We'll still want to have a drainage hole or two in the raised bed, but this won't see nearly as much run-off. This is achieved through the height of the bed, as the raised bed is entirely filled with soil. That means there is more space for fertilizer or water to have to move through before it exits back into the natural environment. That goes a long way to reducing the negative impact that mini-farming could have while keeping it productive as can be.

As a side note, keep in mind that mini-farming techniques can also be applied to tending livestock. Just like crops, mini-farming can reduce the amount of capital and space you need to tend to your livestock. However, it is important to be aware of the dangers of overcrowding your animals. Livestock raised through mini-farming methods aren't necessarily more productive than those raised traditionally, but if you overcrowd them, then you will see a reduction in productivity. Avoid this by being aware of how much space your livestock have. Remember, they are living animals with their own nutritional needs and health concerns. They need to be kept healthy to be productive. So while livestock may not particularly benefit from this one, they certainly do from the next one.

Mini-Farming is More Efficient

MINI FARMING

Efficiency is all about achieving more by doing less. Does this mean there are fewer steps involved in mini-farming when compared to traditional farming? Nope, it is exactly the same in that regard. Of course, there will be variance from farmer to farmer. One person may not like to use any pesticides while another does. These aren't differences in the required steps. They are more like modifications. They are determined by the personal preferences of the individual farmer making the choice, and so, we can disregard the variance they introduce to the equation. But this raises an important question: If there is no notable difference in the steps taken between traditional farming and mini-farming, then just how precisely can mini-farming be described as more efficient?

The answer to that requires we take into account our role in the maintenance and care of our farms. Pretend for a moment that you are about to grow a crop using the traditional approach. The first thing you are going to have to do is till the soil. So you go up and down and create rows. Then you need to seed the bed or the field. Assuming that you aren't using machinery, you are going to need to physically go up and down the field to sow seeds yourself. Of course, you're still going to need to sow seeds when using the mini-farming approach. The difference isn't in the action required there, but in the walking and travel time required to achieve the goal. You need to walk through the field or the bed. But mini-farming uses garden beds that are tightly packed and closer together. Depending on the size of a particular bed, you might not need to do any walking in order to sow the whole thing. While walking might seem like the least of your concerns, the time it eats up can become considerable by the time harvest rolls around. Then you need to go through the field again to harvest all your vegetables, far more time-consuming compared to having them close at hand through intensive gardening techniques.

Another aspect in which the efficiency becomes clear is through our use of raised garden beds as part of our mini-farming toolkit. Raised garden beds will take a little longer to set up since you usually need to build them yourself, but they greatly cut down on the total amount of maintenance and work to be done. A field needs to be tilled between each crop to keep the soil rich and healthy enough for the plants. But a raised garden bed doesn't need to be tilled. The soil is maintained through simple additions of compost before shutting down for the winter. When combined with liquid fertilizer applications, this ensures a nutrient-rich soil without the need to waste energy tilling. Plus, sowing seeds is much easier in a raised bed garden, especially when intensive gardening methods are utilized, because everything is self-contained and easy to access. So here again, mini-farming increases efficiency by cutting time-consuming corners.

This follows through to our livestock as well. If you are raising a bunch of cattle in a large farming operation, then they're either going to be in a tightly regulated barn or out grazing in the fields or the yard. Just like with the larger crops, if you want to check on each of your animals, then this takes up much more time because there is more space in which they can be spread out. But mini-farming reduces the total amount of space and keeps everything closer together. Again, it may seem like a minor detail. It is negligible if you are only cutting out one trip's worth of walking, but the increase in efficiency is best seen by considering the total amount of time saved. It adds up. You can easily save a dozen or more hours in a single season this way. If you continue to farm for several years, then this number can reach into the hundreds or thousands a lot quicker than you might expect.

Mini-Farming Gives You More Control

When it comes to gardening, the best control comes from hydroponics or indoor methods. Growers can fine-tune the environmental factors that have a positive or negative effect on the plants they are growing. This level of control may be present in a mini-farm, as hydroponics can make for a wonderful addition to a mini-farm. But comparing a traditional farm to a hydroponic setup would create a false equivalency. We could say that hydroponics is better than ground-grown farming, but we couldn't use hydroponics to argue for mini-farming as a whole. To do that, we need to compare similar methods. So no hydroponics and no raised beds. This leaves the question: Does mini-farming still give us more control when we use intensive gardening techniques directly in the ground?

The answer is a resounding yes. This harkens back to the second section we looked at in this chapter and the way that mini-farming uses less space. We know that less space allows us to be more efficient, but this isn't the same as control. But it functions on almost the exact idea. The reduction in space makes it easier for the farmer to get at and check each of their plants. By having everything more tightly grouped together, we can get in to check for signs of pests or disease and other issues without as much hassle. This will give us an early warning sign of issues so that we can act quickly and solve them. Thus, mini-farming gives us a higher level of control over the health of our crops. But that isn't all.

One of the more typical ways of maintaining a traditional farm is to use heavy equipment to work the fields. There is something captivating and enjoyable about riding in a tractor, watching how the equipment tills the field, or harvests the plants or fertilizes the soil. A lot of craftsmanship went into the design and creation of these tools. They are also invaluable when it comes to bigger crops because they reduce the amount of time necessary to complete any particular job by a significant amount. But what we save in time we lose in control. We aren't tilling, sowing, fertilizing, or harvesting the field. We're letting the machinery do that. Sure, we're behind the wheel and telling the tractor where to go, but it is the machinery that does the physical work involved. So by turning to this equipment, we hand over our control.

But we've already seen how mini-farming allows us to save time. Even if we weren't walking the larger field, but using a tractor, we would still find ourselves spending more time working the larger field compared to the smaller, mini-farm we've built. So we don't need to worry about time when it comes to mini-farming. That means we don't need to call in the heavy machinery and let it do the job for us. Mini-farming requires us to be directly involved in each of the steps leading to harvest. That allows us to learn more and improve our farming skills, while also giving us full control over the farm and what happens. A piece of heavy machinery such as a harvester might chip a blade and result in a jagged cut that ruins the vegetable, but we will have this experience when we practice mini-farming. If something damages our vegetables, it will be our own doing. We can learn from the mistake so that we don't make it again. Taking over more control means that we gain more experience farming while reducing the frequency of unforeseen problems arising from our reliance on technology.

Mini-Farming is Simple

The best part of mini-farming is that it doesn't take a ton of knowledge in order to get going. You are working with much smaller spaces, and this means there is much less you need to worry about. You are still going to need to know how to check the pH level of your soil or how to clean up after livestock. But the smaller size reduces the need for heavy machinery, and so you won't need to worry about having a tractor license or knowing how to use a combine harvester, for example.

The hardest part of mini-farming is cutting through all of the discussion you'll find on the internet or in most gardening books. If you look at how far apart to space a crop, most books are going to tell you a number in inches or feet that is based on traditional farming. This stands in contrast to intensive farming and mini-farming techniques, and if you go researching without this in mind, then you may be tricked into thinking that you aren't tending to your farm properly. Unfortunately, this is one piece of misinformation that can be quite frustrating. But if you're aware of this pitfall, you'll be prepared.

For the most part, you won't need to go out and seek a whole lot of knowledge. You'll want to learn about the crops or animals you are raising, but you don't need to worry about machinery or the logistics of harvesting a big field and preparing the yield for transportation or storage. These are elements that you'll have to tackle in a miniature form, which makes them far easier. In a way, you could consider mini-farming sort of like a set of training wheels for your farm. Only, you don't actually need to upgrade further down the road. Your mini-farm can be made to turn a constant profit without the next for expansion. So not only is it simpler to get started, but it can remain that simple throughout the rest of your time tending to your mini-farm.

Chapter Summary

- There are a lot of reasons to use mini-farming techniques, most of which are interconnected with each other.

- Traditional farming is an expensive endeavor that only typically makes a profit when it is done on a very large scale. It requires the purchase of land, equipment, seeds, and labor.

- Mini-farming uses less space to grow more plants, doesn't require heavy machinery, and can be harvested by an individual. This all contributes to reducing the amount of capital you need to get started.

- Mini-farming also requires far less space than traditional farming does. Plants may be grown closer together using intensive gardening techniques, or the use of raised garden beds can allow for multiple levels of plants grown on the same spot, thus greatly increasing the number of plants that can be grown.

- Using less space will also lead to less money spent on fertilizer or soil. You will need to use more fertilizer per square foot, but there are less square feet in total, and so the amount will still come out lower, so long as you are growing with productive techniques like rotating crops.

- Traditional farming requires you to have access to the ground itself. A mini-farm can be run through a hydroponic system, and therefore, you could start one indoors if you had to.

- Mini-farms are more productive than traditional farming as it produces more in a smaller area, and this results in bigger yields come harvest time.

- Intensive farming practices can lead to excessive runoff of fertilizers, but combining intensive gardening techniques with sufficiently deep raised garden beds can compensate for this.

- Mini-farming doesn't just refer to crops, but livestock as well. However, livestock will produce far less if they aren't given enough room to live in. You can still raise livestock with mini-farming techniques, but you should be mindful of ensuring they have enough room to stay healthy.

- Mini-farming keeps everything tightly grouped together in a smaller location, which results in a reduction of time spent traveling from plant to plant to take care of them all.

- If you use raised garden beds in your mini-farm designs, then you also remove the need to till the soil, which improves efficiency.

- It's easier and quicker to tend to your livestock when they are kept close together through mini-farming techniques.

- Traditional farming techniques require heavy machinery, and they take away a level of control from the farmer. Mini-farming techniques offer this level of control back and make it easier for farmers to get a hands-on look at precisely how well each plant is growing.

- Mini-farming requires less equipment and therefore has a smaller learning curve, making it a great choice for beginners. The impressive result that mini-farming yields also makes it a terrific choice for experts, too.

In the next chapter, you will learn all about crop farming. We'll look at terms like monocropping, crop rotation, mixed cropping, intercropping, hydroponics, and raised bed gardens in order to see their various advantages and disadvantages. Often, the best mini-farms are those that make use of multiple approaches to balance these pros and cons. By knowing these, you'll be able to design the most effective mini-farm possible.

CHAPTER TWO

CROP FARMING

Despite the fact that we are discussing mini-farming, our available approaches to crop farming are anything but mini. We have just as many, if not more, options available to us when it comes to how we raise the crops in our mini-farm. This is just another reason why this is such a wonderful approach for beginners or experts alike.

In this chapter, we will look at six of the available options we have for growing crops. While we'll look at each of these individually, they are actually broken up into pairs. The first pair is monocropping and crop rotation, which make up two sides of the same coin and deal with how often a crop should be planted. The next pair is mixed cropping and intercropping. These two techniques are often discussed interchangeably, but they are two different approaches to mixing different crop types. The final pair is hydroponic and raised bed crops, which together represent two approaches to how we can go about raising a crop beyond just planting directly in the ground. Every crop is going to either be monocropped or rotated, though not every crop will check off the other four categories. However, a single crop could fit into up to three of these categories (selecting one from each pair). So, while these are all unique, they can be combined if you wish.

Monocropping

Monocropping is the act of continuously growing the same crop in the same field year after year. Of all the categories we look at, monocropping is the one that is the least recommended. That's because it has such a negative impact on the environment. In this regard, it stands in stark contrast to the practice of crop rotation. It still has its supporters, but we are seeing more people discussing how harmful this practice is, and critics of it have even begun to put pressure on major farmers to switch from monocropping to crop rotation. We'll start with the positives so we can see why this technique still has its supporters, but once we turn to the negative, it will be clear why you should never consider monocropping as an option for your mini-farm.

The biggest argument that people make for monocropping is that it is more profitable because it saves money. If you are going to monocrop, then you can really niche down and only buy the equipment necessary to look after that one type of crop. On a larger farm, this can mean an absolutely astounding amount of money saved because the heavy machinery that farms use is costly. Right out the gate, this results in a lower initial investment, and so it is easier to make a profit. Since you plant the same crop every year, you also save money on a recurring basis. You only need to purchase one kind of seed, and you already have the necessary equipment, so the only additional costs for further crops are the seeds, labor, and any mechanical repairs that are needed. This makes monocropping attractive to those who are primarily concerned about earning money. But monocropping has a problem which is far too big to ignore.

That problem comes in the form of the environmental impact that monocropping has. When you grow a single crop in the same soil year after year, the nutrients of that soil are depleted. Eventually, if you tried to grow a crop in this soil, it would just starve to death because it doesn't have the nutrients for healthy growth. Yet this is exactly what monocropping does, and so it becomes necessary for the farmer to use chemical fertilizers to feed the plants. When we talk about issues like fertilizer later in chapter six, we'll be looking at organic fertilizer. Organic fertilizer is weaker than chemical fertilizer because it isn't replacing the nutrients in the soil; instead, it's supplementing them. But monocropping drains away all those soil-bound nutrients, and so it requires a strong fertilizer for the crop to come to harvest. The problem with fertilizers of this strength is that they actually do more damage to the soil and so they only make the problem worse. It's a little like drinking coffee late at night. You might get the energy you need to keep going for a little bit longer, but you are going to crash hard if you don't keep drinking more. Instead of drinking coffee, it is better to sleep. When it comes to our crops, it's better to give the soil a rest through the use of crop rotation. But before we turn our attention to rotating our crops, there's another downside that can't be ignored.

Monocropping exposes your crops to a higher degree of risk of infestation by pests. Most backyard gardeners or indoor gardeners are at risk of pest infestation, but the risk is lessened due to the fact they often use a variety of plants. Not every pest wants to munch on every plant. I might like cake, but you might like pie, despite the fact we're both human. We see the same eating variances within a singular kind of pest as well. Perhaps this is no more clear than when we look at the aphid. Annoying little bugs that they are, aphids actually come in a bunch of different species. Most are named after what they prefer to eat the most, and so we have potato aphids, melon aphids, cabbage aphids and bean aphids to only name a few. If you are monocropping, then you are creating an immense buffet of their favorite food for these pests. In contrast, if you use mixed cropping or intercropping, then you create smaller pockets of the same plant, and this makes it harder for a particular pest to spread through it all.

Likewise, if you practice crop rotation, you will also reduce the frequency of pests. Monocropping plants in the same crop year after year mean your field can become a haven for pests. They can set up shop nearby, so they never have to travel far for a meal. Therefore, you have infestations year after year, and it can be a major headache. To solve this problem, you are going to need to use pesticides, and these contribute further to the negative environmental impact that monocropping has. Rather than just excessive chemical fertilizer in the soil, you end up with excessive amounts of pesticides (which may still be organic but shouldn't be present in such high volumes).

Ultimately, monocropping might save money in the initial investment, but it comes at too high an environmental cost to be recommended. The issues with pests can create a recurring problem that greatly affects your experience and will cut into your profits. If we compare the positive with the negative and then consider the mini-farming approach, we see that for our purposes, monocropping is too much of a negative experience. We don't need to purchase expensive equipment when mini-farming and so we wouldn't be saving money by monocropping. All we would get out of it is low-quality soil and, probably, a lengthy fight against infestation, so we might as well cross out monocropping and push it from our minds.

Crop Rotation

Monocropping, by growing the same crop in the same place, year after year, results in environmental issues and increased struggles with pests. It can also possibly lead to more soil-based disease problems. If we want to avoid these, then we need to make sure we rotate our crops rather than repeat them. Crop rotation requires you to grow more types of plants than monocropping, typically at least three or four kinds. While we will consider crop rotation using a traditional field planting approach, keep in mind that this technique easily adapts to raised beds or other mini-farming approaches to growing.

MINI FARMING

Before we can begin to rotate crops, we need to divide up our field into three or four sections. Often this is done, not within a single field, but across several, so that each field is growing a different kind of vegetable. If we go with four different sections, then we might have lettuce growing in the first, potatoes in the second, carrots in the third, and celery in the fourth. Already this offers a distinct advantage over monocropping through the variety it lets us grow. However, if we grew the same vegetables in each section year after year, then all we have done is monocropped four plants rather than one. What we need to do is rotate the crops. So, if they were in the above order during year one, they would then shift the second year so that the first crop was celery, followed by lettuce, potatoes, and carrots in the second, third, and fourth sections respectively. This would repeat each year until the crops were back to their original space.

Rotating your crops in this way is beneficial because it reduces the frequency of infestation since the parasites aren't given the chance to become accustomed to one particular type of plant in that location. This also has a beneficial effect on the quality of the soil, as different plants soak up different amounts of nutrients. One crop might eat up lots of nitrogen while another prefers to snack on potassium. However, most farmers want to be extremely specific about what they grow in each plot so as to avoid planting members of the same family next to each other. When this happens, there is very little benefit in crop rotation as the same nutrients, pests, and diseases are going to be affected by the change.

When researching crop rotation, you will often find it recommended that you plant a legume, a root veggie, a leafy green, and a fruit-bearing plant in the four crops. This is intended to keep the crops varied, and prevent them falling into the trap we just explored. However, it isn't an ideal guideline to go by because it isn't detailed enough. That can be seen by looking at carrots and parsley. Carrot is a root vegetable, parsley falls into the category of leafy green, so according to the commonly advised method, a crop of parsley could follow after a crop of carrots. But both carrots and parsley are members of the umbelliferae family, and so they soak up similar nutrients while also attracting the same diseases and pests. When dividing up your crops for the purposes of rotating, go by the plant family rather than any loose descriptor such as leafy green or root vegetable.

The biggest downside to crop rotation is that it is more time-consuming than monocropping, and it can also cost much more. This cost is more readily apparent when considering larger farms since mini-farming doesn't require heavy machinery. However, you need to plan out your crop rotations ahead of time and learn how different plant species grow and what needs they have as far as fertilizer, watering, sunlight, temperature, and humidity go. So, while it is healthier to rotate your crops, it is much more involved than monocropping. With that said, I strongly recommend that you rotate your crops as this will keep your soil healthier longer and result in less headaches trying to fight off pests or diseases.

Mixed Cropping

Mixed cropping brings us to the second section of the chapter. Both mixed cropping and intercropping can lend themselves to monocropping, though they also benefit enough from rotating your crops that I am going to categorically advise you to stick to crop rotation in your planning. This section of the chapter should help to dispel some misconceptions around mixed cropping and intercropping since these two methods are often used interchangeably, despite the fact that they are quite a bit different. But they both have the same core idea, which has led to the confusion around them. Regardless of whether you are using mixed cropping or intercropping, each is a way for you to plant two crops in the same field rather than taking two fields to grow the same crop. Of the two, mixed cropping is the most chaotic because the plants being grown share pretty much the exact same space rather than simply sharing the same field.

This method was originally undertaken as a way for farmers to increase the likelihood of their crops making it to harvest. When you are growing food for personal consumption or for business purposes, having a crop fail is the worst thing that could happen. When you are growing to eat, having a crop fail means you might starve. When you are growing for income, having a crop fail means that you aren't going to make the money you need for your bills, or even to support your family and sow the fields the following year. Where we might be out a little money, but can learn from our experience, a failure of this sort could literally be life or death to a farmer. In order to reduce the risk of a crop failing, mixed cropping was used to double the chances of a successful crop making it to harvest. While the same land would be used, it is planted with at least two crops, which means doubling the chances. Some farmers will even go up to three crops in the same field, though it is important to select the right plants. Before we turn to picking our plants, let's take a moment to explore the difference between mixed cropping and intercropping.

The best way to understand what we mean by mixed cropping is to pretend we are about to sow a field with seeds. Normally we would go through the process of tilling the field and getting it into rows. Then, we would take our seeds and either plant them directly in the soil or scatter them about; the method we'd choose would depend on the requirements of the seeds we decide to plant. When we practice mixed cropping, we do the exact same thing. Only this time, we take two types of seeds and sow them at the same time. In a traditional field, this would result in rows that are growing two different types of plants in them. Of course, we aren't necessarily going to be seeding our mini-farms in this same practice, but we can use intercropping the same way. When we grow using a raised bed, we don't need to bother tilling the soil, but we can still spread out two different types of seeds in the same fashion as described here. It is just easier to understand mixed cropping in a traditional sense, as it highlights most clearly how odd this practice seems. Why exactly would mixing your crops together help to create a better harvest?

For that, we need to consider the many reasons a crop fails. Poor temperatures, too much water, too little nutrients, all of these are just some of the reasons. But if each plant prefers different nutrients and has different water requirements, what kills off one plant might actually be beneficial to the other. The result of this is a better chance that one of the crops makes it through to harvest, even if the other crop fails. Unfortunately, this has a bit of a downside to it too. Because these plants are going to be competing for resources, they aren't going to grow as big or bountiful as they would if the crop was only one kind of vegetable. The smaller yield can make this technique undesirable for those who are only growing to earn money, but those who are growing for food can help to prevent themselves from starving this way. But if you do want to give mixed cropping a shot, then it is important that you carefully pick which crops you are going to use.

Picking the right crop isn't very hard, though you do need to take in some considerations to determine what makes for a good pairing. To begin with, you will want to select plants that grow at different heights. Have one that grows taller than the other so that both plants don't need to fight each other for the sunlight. The taller crop is going to get more direct sunlight while the short crop will use the taller crop for shade, so make sure that your shorter crop doesn't require very much direct light. With that said, if you grow a tall crop, then you might want to grow a crop that climbs such as tomatoes, cucumbers, or eggplant, as they can use the taller plant for support. If you are growing three crops in the same field, then pick one that is tall, one that is short, and one in the middle. By doing that, you've created a natural tiering system that allows each plant to get enough sunlight.

You will also want to consider the way the roots of each plant grow. If you are cultivating a plant with a short root system such as lettuce, you wouldn't want to pair it with another plant with a short root system. All that would do is crowd the soil in that particular area and encourage plants to fight each other for resources. It's better to select a plant that grows nice, deep roots to go with one that has shallow roots. While you are considering the needs of the root, also consider how much water each plant needs. If you pick a plant that needs a lot of water, you should pair it with one that doesn't need much at all. What this does is protect you from the two extremes of the elements. Heavy rain might damage the less thirsty plant, but it will keep the thirsty one happy. But the thirsty plant won't be able to survive a drought while the less thirsty one might. The idea of pairing plants based on their needs continues through to their nutrients. If one crop wants nitrogen-rich soil, pair it with one that doesn't need as much nitrogen. By considering the needs of the plants, you can pair them in such a way that they increase their chances of getting to harvest while also not competing too strongly with each other.

If you have picked your crops well, you will see quite a few benefits. For one, if both survive to harvest, then you will have a variety that you wouldn't have otherwise. Of course, one of those crops might fail, but that doesn't mean that the field as a whole has failed. You've created a sort of safety net which would otherwise be absent. Depending on what you decide to grow, this method can actually help to keep your soil richer and for a longer period. Crops that are leguminous, for example, help to keep the nitrogen levels in the soil at healthy levels so you could be improving the soil rather than just draining it. Mixed crops have a tendency to attract less weeds because the way that the plants create a canopy helps to reduce the amount of sunlight that reaches the ground. That means less of this vital resource is being spent helping weeds to grow, and this means less time you spend having to weed the field. Likewise, there are less pests to deal with when you employ mixed cropping because there aren't as many of the same plant grouped together. Pests will prefer to snack on one of the plants rather than both of them, and the confusion that mixed cropping creates in the parasites helps to slow their spread and keep them out of the field in general. Finally, while you are less likely to see an increase in yield, it isn't unheard of. If you have a good year and the crops were chosen in such a manner as to not compete with each other, you may find that you are harvesting more than you expected at the end of the year.

With that said, mixed cropping more often results in a smaller yield. That's one of the reasons people may choose not to use the practice. Mixed cropping also takes a lot more research in order to pull off because you need to not only worry about the needs of one plant, but rather, you must consider the way that two different crops will interact with each other. This makes it a better technique for those who enjoy researching their crops and giving careful consideration to a handful of variables. It is also a lot harder to harvest a mixed crop because you need to be extremely careful. You could damage one of the crops while harvesting the other, and this would destroy the benefits. But if you are looking to maximize the space you have and increase the variety of what you are growing, then mixed cropping might be the right choice for you. But as it is intended for minimizing the dangers of crop failure, if you are looking to increase your yield and potential earnings, then you are better off going with intercropping.

Intercropping

Intercropping is quite similar to mixed cropping except that it separates the space between the different crops you are growing much more clearly. With mixed cropping, we saw that we cultivate seeds from both plants in the same row. Intercropping takes a little more time and dedication to get right. We would start intercropping the same way as we do a regular field or mixed cropping. Once we have our rows lined out, we would then sow the seeds of our first plant in the first row. We'd skip the second row and move to the third row and sow our seeds again. Once we have gone through the whole field this way, we would turn around and go back through it, hitting the even-numbered rows that we originally skipped. This time we would sow the seeds for the second vegetable that we are growing in the field. This would create a pattern of crop 1 - crop 2 - crop 1 - crop 2.

That is what we call row intercropping, as it requires the rows in the first place. But it isn't the only form of intercropping, just the easiest way to grasp the concept. One thing that we could do is to create rows, and then sow the seeds of our main crop in each row. Then we would go back and sow the seeds for our second crop in the middle between the two rows. Yet another way that we could use intercropping is called relay intercropping. Relay intercropping is very specific about when the crops are planted, as the goal is to create a harvest period that lasts much longer than if they were planted at once. Finally, there is also a type of intercropping called mixed intercropping. This approach is a little bit more like mixed cropping, but instead of rows, you have different and varied patterns created from how you plant. Mixed cropping sees the two plants grown together, but mixed intercropping sees the plants grown close together in a way that is beneficial for growth. That might include planting a low and shade-loving plant next to a larger plant that could create a canopy to offer protection from the sun.

This separation between the two plants is the big difference that separates mixed cropping from intercropping. We still need to be extremely careful in considering what plants we are going to grow through this method. While they aren't using the exact same piece of land, they are grown so close together that you still need to take into account a lot of variables. Both plants grown in this method can have shallow or deep roots, as they won't be competing with each other in this fashion, but you will still want to keep them of different sizes in order for each to get enough sun. Most important of all is the way the plants use the nutrients in the soil. If you can balance them so that they aren't soaking up and using all of the same nutrients, then you will have a much easier time bringing the plants to harvest. It should be clear that intercropping uses up more space than mixed cropping, but this space can still be scaled in a similar fashion. When seeding a raised bed, for example, just be careful to sow seeds in straight line patterns so that intercropping is achieved rather than mixed cropping. If you find a few plants have strayed out of their area, then these can be trimmed away to promote better uniformity.

Intercropping takes longer than mixed cropping because you need to be more careful during the sowing stage, but it comes with enough benefits to make it worth it. Your crops will have less problems with weeds. That's because the taller plants will offer shade and make it harder for weeds to get sunlight. Also, the soil will be so busy with so many plants there won't be as much room for weeds to edge in. Intercropping can have more issues with pests than mixed cropping does, but this technique results in fewer pests than regular crops. Pests that prefer the first crop are going to have a hard time navigating through the second crop to get to their next meal. Disease is also less of a problem, especially disease that is found in the soil. Now that we've mentioned the soil, note that it will be able to maintain a much stronger structure due to the different types of organic matter on top. The structure of the soil is even further assisted if you decide to mix crops with different root lengths. This is beneficial for the soil, but it isn't a necessary step the way it is with mixed cropping. Since you balance the nutritional needs of the plants, you can make sure your crops aren't draining the fields. Again, this is made even more effective when you plant a crop like legumes that feed nitrogen back into the soil. Finally, intercropping results in a larger yield than mixed cropping tends to, and this makes it the better choice for those looking to earn money from their crop. So with all of these benefits, it is likely that intercropping is the way you'll want to go if you choose to grow in the soil. Let's take a look at the steps we take to intercrop successfully and then turn our attention over to hydroponics, a water-based approach to growing, and raised bed gardens.

Picking the right plants for intercropping is a lot like picking the right plants for mixed cropping; only there are some important differences that can make or break the whole endeavor. When we use mixed cropping, it is to ensure that one of our plants survives. Since this is the primary goal, we use plants that have quite different needs from each other, so that one of them will be able to survive, no matter if the season is full of heavy rain or a heat-wave drought. But intercropping is used to increase our yield in general. To achieve this, we need our plants to be closer together in their needs, so that we can more readily attend to them and make sure that they are getting what they need. That does leave us open to losing the crop if we plant thirsty plants and then have a drought, or if we plant drought-resistant plants and then have heavy rain. So the risk with intercropping is higher, but it is more in tune with what we would expect out of a traditionally planted crop, and so, while the risk is more than mixed cropping, it is still within the normal range expected by a farmer.

Start by researching the needs of your plants. This is easy enough to do; simply open up Google and search the name of your plant followed by "planting guide," "intercropping," or "nutritional needs." You'll get hundreds of sites with the information you want. First, look at the family that the plant is from. You want to avoid growing plants from the same family. Next, look to see how much water they need. You want them to need roughly the same amount, as you will be watering them together rather than separately. As it can be beneficial to grow plants with root systems of differing lengths, try to get one that is long and one that is short. Of course, you can get away with growing plants of the same size root system because they aren't directly taking up the same space they do with mixed cropping. You need to consider how the size of the plants will affect the sunlight. If you're planting tall plants, you may want to grow them in horizontal rows rather than vertical ones so that they don't throw shade on the short plants. But then again, if you pick shorter plants that prefer the shade, this might be precisely what you want. You may also want to consider planting species that have different growing periods, as having plants that are in different phases can help to reduce how quickly nutrients in the soil are used. Finally, consider making one of the species a legume or another type of plant (such as green manures or accumulators), which helps to keep the soil rich and healthy. If you follow these steps in picking your plants, you can see a major yield.

Harvesting is going to be easier with intercropping compared to mixed cropping, as the plants are spaced out better, and you don't need to worry about damaging one kind while harvesting the other. If you are mindful of your plants and look after them throughout the season, then intercropping can be one of the most effective ways to maximize the use of your space so that your mini-farm can thrive. We've been mentioning fields, but intercropping can be done in a raised bed, which we'll look at now as we turn our attention over to the last section of the chapter.

Raised Garden Beds

A vital component of mini-farming is the maximization of space. This results most often from the fact that we don't have as much space for farming as the major companies do. That pushes us to use practices like intercropping or mixed cropping, as these make better use of the space we have and allow us to grow two (or more) crops in the same area. But before we even begin to start sowing seeds, we should take the time to consider that space and see if we are using it to the best of our ability. One of the most effective approaches that we can use to achieve this is to adopt raised beds into our planning. Out of all of the techniques we've discussed in this chapter, raised beds are the most useful and highly recommended. In fact, frankly, the only way that we can get away with monocropping is through the use of a raised bed. In this section, we'll see why they are so highly recommended, by comparing them to traditional ground-based farming, as well as how we can quickly make one, and the many benefits they provide. But before we even get into them, let me say that raised garden beds should be the cornerstone of your approach to mini-farming.

But what exactly is a raised garden bed? This particular question might seem irrelevant, as the name serves as a description of the product itself. But a raised garden bed is essentially a garden bed that has been raised up above the ground so as to give the gardener more control over the growing environment. In a lot of ways, a raised garden bed is almost like a big plant container. We take a material like wood or stone, and we build four walls, being mindful of the size of the bed. We then fill the raised bed with healthy soil and plant our crop. If done correctly, this gives us a much greater level of control over the growing environment, and this makes it easier to keep the soil filled with nutrients. We can use these raised beds to raise monocrops, intercrops, or mixed crops.

The reason that we can actually achieve a healthy monocrop with a raised bed is directly tied to that level of control. Typically, when growing in a field, you are relying, to a considerable degree, on the soil that is there. We might add some fertilizer to the soil and give it a till or two between seasons, but this only does so much. If we are growing deep-rooted vegetables, then what happens, is the roots grow first through the healthier soil, which we added to the field, until they push into the natural soil that is beneath our added layer. In this approach, we give up control over the soil beyond our top layer. But, in a raised garden bed, we have the option to rely more fully on our soil. We do this by making the raised bed much taller. A raised bed should never be less than half a foot tall, and often, it benefits us to go a foot or even a foot and a half. Since we are the ones that fill it with healthy soil, this lets us control a much greater amount of the growing environment.

Before we look at all of the benefits, let us take a minute to consider how we build a raised bed garden. There are two approaches that differ only slightly, but it is important to consider which approach is more effective. Every raised bed will have four walls around it. These are typically made of wood, but some people may use rocks, bricks, or other materials, including some as wacky as old tires. Since we are growing vegetables to sell for human consumption, we need to be especially careful when it comes to picking a material. Tires, for example, can leak harmful chemicals into the soil, which then degrades the quality of the soil (and the nearby earth), and this can make vegetables grown in a raised bed of this nature pretty unhealthy. So, we must first pick a healthy material such as a hardwood or a non-treated wood. Next, we have to make the biggest decision: do we want to build a bottom for the bed or not? If we only make raised beds that are half a foot or a foot off the ground, then we should probably not add a bottom. That's because we want to make sure our vegetables have enough space for their roots to grow unimpeded. But, by choosing not to add a bottom, we find ourselves reducing the level of control we have over the growing environment because we need to rely on the natural soil underneath it.

I believe it is best to make raised beds with a bottom. The most obvious reason for this is the fact that it lets us keep our control over the growing environment. If we have a raised bed that is tall enough, there is enough room for the roots of any vegetable to grow, and this means that we don't need to cross our fingers and hope the soil is good. We'll see in a moment how we control the soil and keep it nice and healthy enough to achieve a monocrop. But, the other reason for including a bottom, is that it helps reduce the incidence of burrowing pests getting into our crop. While approaches like intercropping and mixed cropping can reduce pests such as aphids or whiteflies, they can't completely protect us from critters. A raised bed with a bottom does, as it becomes much harder for them to get in. It should be noted that, while it is harder for them, it's not impossible. That's because the inclusion of a bottom does not entirely cut off the raised bed from the natural soil. We need to be careful to ensure that our raised beds have enough drainage capability so as not to trap water and moisture in the bed. Trapped moisture makes it more likely that we'll drown our crop and lead to diseases such as root rot. We need to drill in a few drainage holes in the raised bed. We use a mesh covering over these holes to make it harder for things to get in, but the fact that there are holes at all makes it a possibility, albeit a rare one.

The biggest downside this approach has is that we need to build our raised garden beds. It requires a little bit of investment, as we need to acquire materials, as well as the knowledge necessary to put the bed together. It is also necessary we keep in mind that the larger the bed, the more securely it needs to be built as the soil we fill it with puts pressure on the foundation, and it could easily break one that is made cheaply or poorly. This investment of money, time, and energy may leave you thinking that you're better off skipping over raised garden beds, but that would be a mistake. Making the raised bed may take up a lot of time, but once it is made, it is far easier to maintain crops in a raised bed garden, as well as the soil itself. When you are considering using a raised bed approach for your mini-farm, remember not to design the beds to be too wide. We want to be able to reach all of our plants, and so we should never make raised beds that are wider than four feet. They can be as long as you want, but the width should be capped at four feet maximum.

So, there is only one major downside to using raised beds in your mini-farm, but what about the possible benefits? These far outweigh the negatives, so much so that it isn't even fair to compare the two. It would be like comparing Shaquille O'Neal to someone who just picked up a basketball for the first time in their life. These benefits include the level of control we have, specifically over the soil, a reduction in pests and critters, less strain on our backs, fewer weeds, more space, and an earlier start to the growing season. If you are looking to maximize your potential profits, then that last point is going to be especially interesting to you. We'll take a look at each of these now, and then turn our attention over to the chapter's final section on hydroponics.

Let's start with that control. To begin with, we choose the soil that fills our raised beds. This allows us to ensure that we are picking soil with plenty of nutrients. At the end of the growing season, after we have harvested our plants, we need to prep our raised beds to ready them for the winter. While the easiest way to do this would be to cover them with a tarp, we can repair the soil by covering the beds with a layer of compost followed by a layer of mulch. The compost will decompose over the course of the winter so that, by the time the new season comes around, the nutrients have been able to permeate the soil and keep it as healthy as it was when we first used it. It is through this act of winter preparation that we keep our soil fertile enough to be able to monocrop if we so choose.

Because the soil is raised and kept separate from the natural soil below, we reduce the incidence of weeds, pests, and disease. We may still find pests in our raised beds, but they have a much harder time getting there, and we can even use a ring of cinnamon around the edge of the bed to make it that much harder for pests to get in. Diseases like root rot or nutrient burn are still pretty standard in raised beds, but this is because they primarily happen due to the way the farmer has acted rather than just occurring naturally. Root rot happens when we overwater our plants, and nutrient burn happens when we feed them too much fertilizer. But, if we take diseases caused by our actions out of the picture, raised beds have far, far fewer problems with disease than traditional crops do. They also don't cause as many problems with weeds. When growing a crop normally, we need to till the soil of the field before planting each year. Doing this pushes around weed seeds and assists them in spreading out over our fields. Raised beds don't require any tilling, and so we don't move these seeds around as much. We also use a mulch covering during the winter, which helps to prevent weed seeds from getting into the bed, and this also blocks those that are present from getting enough sun and water to grow. Fewer pests and weeds, and less disease, means you don't need to devote as much time to saving your crop. You can have more time to literally enjoy the fruits of your labor.

Since we can design our raised beds in such a way as to create multi-level tiers, we can make the most out of the space we have. Even when we don't create multi-leveled setups, we can plant our crops closer together in a raised bed when compared to the same crop directly in the earth. That's fantastic because we want to make sure that our mini-farms are as productive as possible. But the greatest benefit of using raised beds in this fashion isn't one that affects your crops, but rather one that affects you. Since mini-farming doesn't use the same equipment as a larger farm, harvesting tends to mean getting down on your hands and knees to get to the same level as the plants. If you have bad knees or a bad back, then this can be the most miserable part of the whole experience. But a raised bed reduces the amount of strain that you need to put on yourself. With that said, this does affect certain vegetables such as potatoes. When harvesting potatoes, it is easy to damage them and thus reduce your overall profits. But raised beds make it easier to control the harvest and reduce damage such as this.

Speaking of profits, if you are farming for income, then a raised bed may help you to earn more. Because it is raised off the ground, these garden beds begin to warm up earlier in the year when compared to a traditional field. That means you can get your crops planted earlier. They also hold onto heat longer, so that you can get upwards of two extra weeks growing out of them at the end of the season. If you are raising a crop that can be harvested multiple times a year like lettuce, this can be enough time to fit another crop into the year. When growing in the ground, we can typically get two full harvests from lettuce. We can easily get three and sometimes even four harvests when growing the same crop in a raised bed.

So if you are looking to start a mini-farm, there is no better approach than to use raised beds. However, this assumes you have enough space outside in order to grow. There are some of us who don't have that space. While you might think that means you can't start your own mini-farm, this isn't true at all. You can still mini-farm even if all you have access to is a spare room in your house. You just need to use the right method. It is this method we turn to now.

Hydroponics

When it comes to farming, we almost always need to select crops that are native to our area or to an area with similar environmental factors such as sunlight, temperature, and humidity. That isn't automatically a limiting factor, as there are so many different kinds of vegetables, herbs, and fruits that we can raise in any environment. So, we still have a lot of variety, but we can't grow everything. At least, we can't grow everything when we rely on traditional farming methods or even raised bed gardens. Most of the time, when we talk about growing crops, what we are discussing is growing crops outdoors and thus relying on that environment. But hydroponics offers us a way of, not only fully controlling our growing environment, but also to grow our crops indoors. You can grow a healthy and bountiful crop in the comfort of your own home through hydroponics. But, with that said, you should keep in mind that hydroponics is also being used more often to raise full crops within greenhouses. This is excellent because it shows that we can scale up a hydroponic growing operation as our mini-farms prove to be profitable. Out of all the approaches that we have looked at, hydroponics is the most unique. We'll take a look at what it is, the different setups we can use, the pros and cons that come with it, and even how to quickly set up the simplest of hydroponic systems so that you'll see that it's easier than you might think.

Hydroponics offers a way of growing crops without using soil. If you have never heard of this approach before, then this might seem a little crazy. In traditional farming, you plant your seeds in soil. This soil has nutrients in it already, but we also fertilize our plants on a regular basis to make sure they don't run out throughout the growing season. In hydroponics, we don't use soil, and we don't use fertilizer. Instead, we use a nutrient solution. We basically just take a tub of water and then add liquid or dissolvable nutrients into it to create the perfect, nutritional blend for our plants. Our plants are then grown in an inert growing medium such as coco coir. This medium acts like soil in order to help our plants stay firm and supported, but it has no nutrients in it. Instead, the roots of the plants are allowed to grow out of the medium and dangle down into the nutrient solution. This may be achieved by having the roots dangle into the nutrient reservoir itself, or by having them dangle over a running stream of the solution. We may also use a top-down method to pump the nutrient solution over the inert growing medium so that it feeds through the medium to the plant's roots, and then back into the nutrient reservoir. This creates a closed system. Beyond the significant benefit of being able to grow plants indoors, this approach wastes less water than traditional growing methods, and there is less potentially harmful runoff.

One of the issues with hydroponics is that certain items are much more difficult to build and require much more money when compared to traditional crop farming methods. For example, when we grow a crop traditionally, all of the light is provided by the sun. Hydroponics requires us to purchase LCD grow lights in order to supply this for our plants artificially. That means we need to invest in lights and then continue to pay the power bill. It also means the lights have to continue to work. Some setups also require us to use an airstone to keep enough oxygen in the reservoir so that the roots of our plants don't just drown. Others need an air pump to push the nutrient solution through the various pipes so all of our plants can get their necessary nutrients. While this requires us to invest in these parts and use more electricity, they also create moving parts that can break down. If a part of a hydroponic system breaks down and isn't fixed quickly, you can easily lose a whole crop in a short amount of time. So when we look at disadvantages, we see that these systems require us to spend more money, devote more time to maintenance, and we also need to learn how to build them. With cons like this, you might think it is hard to recommend hydroponics, but it wouldn't be in this book if there weren't equally as many benefits.

One of the biggest benefits of hydroponics is obviously the fact that we can grow whole crops indoors through this approach. If you only have access to an inside location, then this is terrific. But if you have access to both an indoor location and an outdoor one, then you may still want to consider hydroponics as it allows you to increase how much you harvest each year. With traditional farming, we raise our crops during the growing season and then harvest them before the winter. During the winter, we are left waiting for warmer weather before we can get back out and sow the new crop. With hydroponics, since we entirely control the growing environment that a crop exists in, we can keep growing throughout the winter. Out of everything that we've looked at so far, hydroponics offers us the best way to increase our income because we no longer need to take a quarter of the year off. If you are growing for profit, this is amazing. But, if you are growing to feed your family, this is even better.

Another fantastic reason to use a hydroponic system is the fact that hydroponics produces larger vegetables and a bigger yield. A larger yield means more money, and so it should be clear why this is desirable. But often, when talking about traditional farming, we equate a larger yield to the use of chemical fertilizers. The use of these chemical fertilizers often leads to harmful runoff getting into nearby soil or waterways, as well as a reduction in the taste of the vegetables grown. Hydroponics is a closed system, and so there is no runoff. There is also no need to add any fertilizers to the mixture, as everything that the plants need is already in our nutrient solution. What's more, hydroponics helps us to produce tastier vegetables. There's been a lot of research done on this regarding lettuce, but the most impressive finding concerns herbs. Herbs can be a very profitable crop to grow, and when grown in a hydroponic system, they are up to 30% more aromatic. This means they smell and taste much stronger than herbs grown in the soil.

Hydroponic systems also rarely have to deal with pests or diseases. Most agricultural diseases are soil-based, and since hydroponics completely removes soil from the equation, those diseases are gone as well. Pests can still be a problem, but since most hydroponic systems are built indoors, it isn't simple for pests to get at them. To make sure this remains true, farmers need to be mindful to wash their hands and not bring outside pathogens into their growing area by accident. Farmers also need to remove any dead plant matter that's fallen off from their crops as this creates a place for disease and pests to grow. So long as the safety and cleanliness of the growing space are maintained, pests and disease shouldn't be a problem. You do need to be careful to ensure that your nutrient reservoir is closed properly, as water-based diseases might be an issue. However, these diseases are easy to avoid with just a little bit of consideration and an awareness of hygiene.

So, we've referred to systems in the plural rather than the singular. This is because there are several types of hydroponic systems that you can create and use. Which system is best suited for your needs is going to be determined by what you are trying to do. You can get away with a very simple system if you are growing a crop like lettuce, but you'll want a more complex system for raising tomatoes. You also need to be aware that hydroponics isn't a great match for every vegetable. Potatoes and root vegetables will still need to be grown directly in soil instead. We close out this chapter by taking a quick look at the six most common hydroponic systems, and then see how easy it is to build the seventh system, which is mentioned less but is a great fit.

The six main hydroponic systems are the nutrient film technique system, the deep water culture, the wick system, the ebb and flow system, the drip system, and the aeroponics system. There is also what we call aquaponics, which is a hydroponic system that uses live fish to create the necessary nutrients for our plants. Aquaponics is beyond the scope of our conversation, but if you are looking to maximize your use of space, then it can allow you to raise fish for sale alongside your crops.

A nutrient film technique uses an airstone and water pump to push the nutrient solution through a tube to wash over the roots of the plants. The plants are grown in baskets with slits that allow the roots to come out, and the baskets are placed in an angled tray. The tray is angled so that water flows back into the nutrient reservoir. This method washes the roots with water, but doesn't keep them in it or feed water through the growth medium. This makes the nutrient film technique the polar opposite of the deep water culture. The deep water culture has the plants grow in the same type of basket, but now the basket hangs directly into the nutrient reservoir. Normally we would be worried about the plants drowning, but an airstone provides the roots with plenty of oxygen.

Both the wick system and the ebb and flow system introduce the nutrient solution directly into the growing medium. The wick system is among the easiest systems to make, as wicks made out of nylon are run between the nutrient reservoir and the growing medium. The wick method is best used for crops like herbs or lettuce. The ebb and flow system works on a timer so that every so often, a water pump turns out and pumps water over the growing medium. The water then slowly drains through the medium and back into the nutrient reservoir. The drip system works like the ebb and flow system, but instead of flooding the growing medium, it slowly drips nutrient solution on top throughout the day and night.

The most complicated set up out of these is the aeroponics one. The plants hang down into the reservoir, but the water level is low enough so that the roots don't dangle directly into it. Instead, a water pump is used to push the water through nozzles that spray mist onto the roots. Out of all the systems we looked at, this is the most complicated and prone to breaking, and I do not really advise this for beginners.

If you are looking to start growing crops in a hydroponic system, then consider starting with lettuce in a Kratky method system. It's similar to the deep water culture in that the roots of the plant dangle down. But we typically refill a deep water culture, and we need to use an airstone to introduce oxygen to the roots. The Kratky method allows the roots to dangle down, but it is designed to be built and then left alone. The roots of the plants suck up the nutrient solution. Rather than filling the reservoir up, the roots are allowed to drain it so that there is more open air for them to get oxygen. By the time all of the nutrient solution has been absorbed, the plants are ready for harvest. All you need to set this system up is to take a container and fill it with nutrient solution, then cut holes in the top so that you can stick a mesh plant container into it. This method can result in lettuce that is 30% larger than traditionally grown lettuce, and yet it is as easy as can be.

What Approach is Right For Me?

If you are unsure of which method to use to grow your crops, there are a few simple questions you can ask yourself.

Are you growing indoors or outdoors? If you are growing indoors, then you will have to select the hydroponic approach.

Are you growing in the ground directly or in a raised bed? I suggest using raised beds whenever possible, but this isn't always the case.

Once you know the answer to the previous question, you can more easily figure out if you should use intercropping, mixed cropping, or monocropping. If you are growing in the ground directly, monocropping is out.

To choose between mixed cropping and intercropping, you should first set out your goals with your mini-farm. If you are looking to keep yourself fed, then you will probably want to go with a mixed cropping approach. If you are looking to earn money, intercropping is best.

Remember to rotate your crops every year if you are growing directly in the ground. If you are growing in raised beds, monocropping a profitable plant is possible.

Once you have the answers to these questions, you can start to plan your mini-farm and get to researching which plants make for the best combinations. If you still aren't sure what you should be growing, stick around for the next chapter where we look at profitable crops.

MINI FARMING

Chapter Summary

- There are many different approaches that we can take to raising crops. Each has its pros and cons and should be considered carefully.

- Monocropping is the act of growing the same crop in the same field, again and again.

- Monocropping is the most harmful of the practices that we can use to grow. It drains the health of the soil and requires chemical treatments to promote growth.

- People that argue for monocropping point out that it is more profitable because you don't need to purchase any extra equipment.

- Monocropping is so harmful to the environment that multiple world governments have outright banned it in the agricultural sector.

- Monocropping increases the risk of pests and disease.

- In contrast to monocropping, crop rotation is the act of planting a different crop in your field each year. Doing so allows the soil to stay healthier, and certain crops are even good at returning nutrients to the soil.

- Crops should be rotated on a three to four-year basis so that there are two or three different types planted before you get back to the original crop.

- Make sure that the crops you plant are all in different families. Planting two vegetables from the same family will defeat the purpose of crop rotation.

- Crop rotation takes more time than monocropping, but it is much healthier and results in bigger yields and better soil.

- Mixed cropping is often confused with intercropping, as both focus on growing more than one crop in the same field.

- Mixed cropping grows both crops in the same row, while intercropping grows two crops next to each other in close proximity.

- Mixed cropping is primarily used to increase the chances that one of the crops survives to harvest. It results in a smaller yield, but it can prevent a farmer from having nothing at all by winter.

- Plants are chosen for mixed cropping because of their differences. If one crop has shallow roots, then you plant it with a crop that has deep roots. If one crop likes dry conditions, you plant it with a crop that likes wet conditions. This helps to ensure that one of the crops makes it to harvest.

- Mixed cropping results in less issues with pests, disease, and weeds. This method also helps to promote healthier soil, too.

- Mixed cropping isn't as good if you are concerned with profits rather than consumption.

- Intercropping grows crops nearby to each other and offers almost all the same benefits as mixed cropping. The major difference is that intercropping results in larger yields.

- Intercropping is a longer process than mixed cropping, as you need to be careful when sowing the crops.

- Make sure that you carefully research the needs of the plants you are putting together. You want mixed crops to have contrasting needs and intercrops to have similar needs.

- Raised garden beds offer the best way of maximizing your space, and you should definitely be using them if you are mini-farming.

- Raised beds are garden beds that have been lifted off the ground by several inches to several feet. You then fill the raised bed with healthy soil, and it lets you have a much greater level of control over the growing environment.

- Since we control the soil in our raised beds, we could monocrop with them if we wanted to and not have to worry about damaging the soil.

- Raised beds are shut down for the winter with a layer of compost that adds healthy nutrients back into the soil for the following spring.

- Making a raised bed garden is time-consuming and the biggest downside to using them. You need to build them securely and make sure to use materials that won't poison your crop.

- Raised beds have fewer problems with soil degradation, weeds, pests, and disease.

- Raised beds can also be designed to be multi-level, and this lets us grow twice as many vegetables in the same space.

- Hydroponics uses a nutrient solution rather than soil to grow plants. It is also the only way for us to grow crops indoors.

- When herbs are grown in a hydroponic system, they are 30% more aromatic. Leafy greens like lettuce also show a roughly 30% increase in yield when produced hydroponically.

- Hydroponic systems cost more money than any of the other approaches, but they offer us the most control possible. Being indoors, they also don't have issues with pests very often.

- We can easily scale up a hydroponic operation, and there are enough of a variety of systems that we can choose an easy one to begin with.

- Potatoes and other root vegetables can't be grown in a hydroponic system.

- To decide which of these approaches is right for you, consider the space that is available to you to grow and what your goals are.

In the next chapter, you will learn all about which crops are the most profitable. Vegetables like potatoes, tomatoes, cabbages, and onions will be discussed to see how they are grown, harvested, and processed either for storage or sale. What's most profitable for you to grow will depend on the supply and demand in your local area, so consider visiting a local farmers' market to find out what is best for you.

CHAPTER THREE

PROFITABLE VEGETABLES TO GROW

In this chapter, we're going to learn what it takes to grow some of the more profitable vegetables there are. We'll also be taking a moment to discuss why you should consider adding herbs to your mini-farm, as these little plants are surprisingly profitable. Keep in mind that knowing what plants are most profitable for your mini-farm depends on the market value in your local area. The simple economics of supply and demand are at play here. If your local area has an abundant supply of potatoes, they aren't going to be nearly as profitable for you as they are for someone else. To get a sense of what is being offered locally, head to your nearest farmers' market and see what is being sold. You may want to take a pen and paper with you so you can keep track of everything you see. Write down what vegetables are being offered, how large of a supply there is, and what they are selling for.

You can use this information to figure out if you can earn a profit selling alongside these other farmers, or if you should specialize in a crop that is under-represented.

We'll take a look at potatoes, tomatoes, cabbages, and onions in this chapter. We'll see what conditions they need to grow, how to ensure a healthy crop, and how to make money selling them down the road. Herbs will also earn a special mention in this chapter, along with the way that we can expand what we offer for sale without having to expand the crops we plant. This little trick might seem like common sense when you hear it, but you'd be amazed at how many farmers don't consider this simple way of expanding their products and income.

Growing Potatoes

Potatoes are an excellent crop because they lend themselves to many different recipes. They can be baked, mashed, fried. You can eat them as a side dish to most meals, or you can add some spices and fry them for homemade chips. They are such a staple of most people's diets that there is almost always a demand for them. They're also incredibly filling, which makes them a good choice for those whose mini-farms are primarily set up in order to feed their families. Potatoes are quite easy to grow and can net a decent profit, so long as you are careful when it comes to harvesting. Keep in mind that while you can grow potatoes in a raised bed garden, they aren't fit for being grown in a hydroponic system, and so those indoor farmers reading this might want to skip over this section. A vegetable like tomato, lettuce, or cabbage is more suited for the indoor approach.

Potatoes like to be grown in cooler weather rather than hot weather. However, they still go into the ground around the middle of April, after the last frost of the year has happened. This is important, even if you are using a raised bed garden. A frost can kill off your plants before they get a chance to begin, so never plant before the last frost. If you are absolutely desperate to get them started earlier, then you can risk planting them and use a tarp to protect them from frost, but this doesn't guarantee they'll survive. Rather than worry about starting mid-April, use a thermometer to check the temperature of the soil, and use this as your basis for when to plant. You want a temperature of at least 50F before you go ahead and sow your seeds.

Potatoes should be grown in soil that's loose, as they need to push their way through it. As potatoes grow, they'll push the soil away from them. If your soil is too tight, they won't be able to achieve this, and you'll end up harvesting tiny potatoes. Make sure that the location gets a minimum of six hours of sunlight out of the day. When planting in rows, they should be three feet apart from each other. Those planting in raised beds will be able to get away with a much smaller amount of space between each.

Potato seeds like to have about a foot between each other, and they like to be covered with a couple of inches of soil after they have been planted. Remember to water the seeds immediately after planting. If the conditions are right, then you should start to see seedlings poking through the soil after about two weeks. As potatoes grow, it is important that you do what is called hilling. Around the sprouting seedlings, parts of the potato will be visible at first. Push the soil up and around the seedling to cover this part. This creates little hills of soil around each potato plant. It's a necessary process since sunlight could cause damage to the crop and produce inedible potatoes.

If you are growing small potatoes on purpose, then you can expect to harvest three weeks after the seedlings begin to flower. For fully-grown potatoes, you want to wait until the foliage on top of the soil has fallen over and died. You might see this and think there is a problem with your crop, but it means they are fully-grown and almost ready to be pulled from the soil. Give them two weeks before harvesting, as this allows the skin of the potato to harden up and take on the texture that we associate with healthy potatoes. Keep in mind that waiting too long will result in a loss of the crop, so never wait more than two weeks after the foliage dies. While you usually water potatoes once every five days, you should slow down your watering as it gets closer to harvest. Reducing the water allows the potatoes to grow more firm and solid, the way that we expect potatoes to be.

When it is time to harvest, pick a dry day, and be extremely careful digging into the soil. Potatoes can be anywhere in the soil, as they have small cords that connect them to the foliage on top. If you were growing carrots, you could see that the carrot is directly connected to the foliage. But since potatoes aren't, they are able to spread out in the soil, and so often they aren't directly beneath the foliage at all. When digging into the soil, it becomes very easy to suddenly chip into a potato and damage it to the point that it can no longer be sold. Make sure that you bring your potatoes in from the sun, as this can cause them to taste to turn green and take on a bitter taste. You will want to store potatoes for at least two weeks in a location with a temperature between 45F and 60F. After they have been given enough time to cure like this, you can take them to the market to sell. This curing will let them stay fresh for a longer time, so you don't have to worry about your crop rotting before it sells. Just make sure that you never store them in a refrigerator, as this will shorten their lifespan. Also, don't wash your potatoes but instead use a brush in order to remove the dirt. Washed potatoes also have a shorter lifespan, so only wash potatoes when you are using them in a meal.

If you follow these steps, then potatoes can last a decent amount of time, and this makes them one of the crops that are great for starting out. When you are beginning, and just judging the interest, you might find that potatoes aren't in high demand and they don't sell as quickly as you expected. Since they can last a long time, you are more likely to sell them all off in the long run when compared to another vegetable, which only has a short shelf life.

Growing Tomatoes

Tomatoes can be a riskier crop. They require a lot more upkeep when compared to potatoes. They also don't keep as long in their natural form, and so it is a good idea to confirm there is a demand for them prior to planting. With that said, tomatoes also offer a way of creating more products down the line. We'll look at using tomatoes in this way later in the chapter.

It takes between 60 and 80 days for tomatoes to grow, which means they have a long growing season, and this can reduce the overall profit you make. For example, you could grow two batches of lettuce in this same timeframe. However, tomatoes tend to sell at a higher price than lettuce, and so it can be worth it. But if you run into a problem with your tomatoes, you are going to have lost a lot of time.

Tomatoes should be grown in a location that gets full sun. They should have a minimum of six hours each day and a maximum of twenty-four. That's right, tomatoes like the sun so much that they could soak it up all day long if they wanted. This is worth noting because we can grow tomatoes in our hydroponic systems; however, they would eat up a lot of electricity. If grown in soil, make sure the soil is loose so that it drains quickly and that it has a pH level of 6.5.

Tomatoes are grown in a grid-like pattern rather than in rows. Plant tomatoes two feet apart from each other in all directions. Tomatoes grow on vines, and so we have to provide them with a trellis to prevent them from just dragging across the dirt. Set these up when you are planting, so that you can start to use them as soon as the tomatoes need them. You can expect to see seedlings growing up after a couple of weeks, but most people start theirs indoors and transplant them into the field after about two months. You will want to prepare the soil to have lots of phosphorus to grow big and beautiful tomatoes. However, keep the nitrogen level of the soil lower as they don't enjoy nitrogen very much and will quickly burn themselves out on it if you're not careful.

Tomatoes need to be watered more often than most vegetables. Make sure to water them deeply so that it promotes a healthy root system. Tomatoes should be watered right up until the time they are ready to harvest. Unlike many vegetables, tomatoes can be kept on the vine for an indefinite period of time. You'll want to harvest before the first winter frost, but otherwise, it is best to leave them on the vine for the longest period possible. You'll know they are ready to harvest because they'll have the bright red color of a healthy tomato while also being firm when squeezed. Some tomatoes may fall off before this happens. If this is the case, pick up the fallen tomatoes and put them into a bag in a dark room with a cool temperature. This can help them to continue to ripen and reduce the amount of waste the crop produces. To harvest, simply pick the tomatoes off the vine.

Make sure that you don't put new tomatoes into the refrigerator. Doing that increases their lifespan, but it reduces their flavor. Instead, try to sell your tomatoes as quickly as possible. If they aren't selling quickly enough, then stick around for another way to make a profit from this crop.

Growing Cabbage

Cabbage, like lettuce and other leafy greens, is among the healthiest options we can pick to consume. It also lends itself to multiple harvests in the growing season, and that means a better chance at making a solid profit. Cabbage also lends itself to hydroponics and, when grown by that method, shows a major increase in size when compared to traditionally-grown cabbage. It used to be a tradition in Ireland that you would plant cabbage on St. Patrick's Day. While we can start cabbage then, it is better to start cabbage seeds indoors and wait three or four weeks before transplanting them outside. That allows you to begin before the last frost so that your transplanted cabbages can get a head start growing.

Anytime you can get a head start, that means a larger possible income when harvest comes.

Cabbages are hungry plants, which means that they soak up all of the nutrients in the soil very quickly. You are going to need to fertilize cabbage regularly; otherwise, they will suffer from stunted growth. When transplanting, you typically want to leave a foot or two between each plant. How much room you leave is dependent on the size of the cabbage you are looking to grow. If you are looking to produce smaller heads, then you can plant them closer together and be ready to harvest them earlier. But larger heads require more space so they can stretch out and develop as they should. Keep in mind that even small heads of cabbage should be kept about a foot apart. This is due to the way, when they're too close, they compete with each other, eat up all the nutrients, and the result is smaller yields. If you are growing regular-sized cabbages, then you can expect two harvests in the year. If you are growing smaller ones, you should be able to squeeze in a third harvest.

To grow cabbages, you are going to want to feed them an NPK balanced fertilizer for the most part, but three weeks after they are in the ground, you also need to add some nitrogen into the soil. Nitrogen promotes foliage growth, and, since leafy greens are composed of foliage, nitrogen is the Holy Grail of nutrients necessary for large plants. You can expect to apply the NPK balanced fertilizer on a weekly basis. If you are growing full-sized cabbage, then expect it to take ten weeks before harvesting. Each plant should harvest about two pounds worth of product.

Harvesting cabbage should be done when it is dry out. Take a clean knife and carefully cut away any yellow leaves. Green leaves should be kept on, even if they are loose and don't seem very appetizing. These leaves help to keep the cabbage fresh while you store it. If you don't feel comfortable using a knife, you can always remove the full plant from the soil, and then hang it in a moist, dark location that is close to freezing. If you remove the heads properly, however, you only need to keep them in the shade. You can get a second crop, without having to sow any more seeds, by removing the head of the cabbage but leaving the leaves in place. This encourages the plant to grow a new head. These new heads will be much smaller than the original and are, what we call, microgreens. They aren't as profitable, but they can be just as delicious. When you are entirely done with the crop, it is important to remove all of the plant matter and the roots from the soil. If you neglect this, they will only promote the growth and spread of disease.

Cabbages should be wrapped in plastic and stored in the refrigerator. They can be expected to last two weeks this way. If you have a dark, dry location in your house like a cellar, then you can keep cabbages fresh for close to three months. Cabbages can be a very profitable crop, but it is crucial that you sell them quickly. You don't want to end up with a lot of rotting heads and no choice other than to throw them away.

Growing Onions

An easy crop to grow, onions might make you cry when they're peeled, but they'll make your bank account smile as you sell off this profitable crop. We start to grow onions when the soil is 50F, or the seeds we sow won't germinate and take hold. Since onions primarily grow in the soil, we want to make sure that we use a loose and quick-draining soil the same way that we do for potatoes. Onions are another vegetable that benefits from adding some extra nitrogen into the soil near the start of their lifecycle. With onions, you can add nitrogen at the same time as you sow their seeds. It is important to practice crop rotation with onions, as they usually deplete the nutrients from the soil. They aren't quite as bad for it as cabbages are, but they are certainly very hungry plants.

MINI FARMING

When planting onions from seed, keep in mind that their seeds do not live very long. You want to make sure you only purchase the freshest of seeds and get them into the ground quickly. Onions are generally grown half a foot apart in rows that are a foot to a foot and a half apart. Despite the fact that they primarily grow in the ground in the fashion of a root vegetable, producing onions has more in common with growing leafy greens. You'll want to provide them with a nitrogen fertilizer every couple of weeks, as this promotes large bulbs to grow. Once the onions begin to grow large, and the soil around them starts to fall away, you no longer need to fertilize them. Also, unlike potatoes, you don't want to create hills around your onions. When the soil falls away, let it stay that way.

Onions don't need to be watered frequently. If you have a layer of mulch on the soil, they'll need to be watered even less often. Typically, you can expect to water them about once a week. Just make sure that you don't forget. Onions are a little tricky, in that they could be going through a drought and still look perfectly healthy. But looks can be deceiving. Make sure that you set a watering schedule and don't let the dates slip your mind. You want your onions to *be* healthy and tasty, and not just look healthy while they are still in the ground.

As onions grow, you might notice that some of them start to send up flower stalks. When you see this happen, immediately harvest those onions. These aren't fully matured, but they have stopped growing. The onions harvested in this manner aren't going to be good to sell, as they only last a day or two. But you can consume them without any detrimental effects, so they don't have to go to waste. Mature onions have foliage that turns yellow and then falls over. When this happens, you can step on the stalks to speed up the process. Brush soil back away from the bulb, and then pull them from the soil once the tops turn brown instead of yellow. To store, you will need to remove the roots and cut the dry top off to about an inch from the top of the bulb. Onions can cure outside, just sitting on the soil, for a couple of days before being brought inside. Once inside, they'll still need to dry for about two weeks before being stored at around 40F. Onions can last for a long time, so you will be able to sell a crop for a few months after harvesting.

Growing Herbs

While there are too many herbs for us to look at each of them, it is worthwhile to note that these are among the most profitable crops you can grow. Basil, cilantro, chives, and ginseng are all among the most profitable crops that you can raise. If you are looking to earn money first and foremost, then you shouldn't neglect raising herbs alongside your vegetables.

Growing herbs doesn't take much work at all. You can and should grow them in a hydroponic system, as this will result in much more effective and appealing plants. Herbs are 30% more aromatic when grown hydroponically. While many hydroponic systems can be quite complicated to set up, herbs can be grown in a mini Kratky method system to great effect. Simply get yourself a small container with a tight lid, fill it with a nutrient solution, and place the herbs inside. Most hydroponic systems benefit from being grown indoors, but the Kratky system entirely cuts off the reservoir from the outside world, and you never need to open it. That means it works quite well when left outside in the sun. Make sure that the container you use isn't see-through, as direct sunlight hitting the nutrient solution will promote the growth of algae, and this will prevent the roots of the herbs from reaching the solution and getting the nutrients they require.

Herbs make for a wonderful addition to any mini-farm because they're quite small. You can easily grow a small batch of herbs without taking up any space at all. But if you are able to sell them and make a good income, it is simple to scale up a herb operation. You can also grow herbs all year round. Research which herbs grow the best in your local environment, and set aside at least one square foot of space to grow them. When you see how much money they can bring in, you'll be thankful you took the time to invest in them.

Jams and Salsas

We close out the chapter not on a vegetable, but one of the products that we can make out of them. Fruits and vegetables don't last nearly as long as we would like. If we aren't able to sell off our tomatoes quickly enough, then we either need to toss them out or eat them up. If we are growing primarily for an income, then this is a serious disappointment because both options mean we are making less money than we expected.

One way we can get around this issue is to make jams or salsas out of our vegetables. This doesn't work for every vegetable, but we can use some creativity to make delicious and natural mixtures like this to sell alongside our fresh vegetables. Plus, if you take the time to learn how to bottle a salsa, you can use that skill to process your vegetables and bottle them for longer storage. Jars of vegetables don't sell as well as fresh ones do, but jars of jam and salsa can be useful sources of income so long as you use a tasty recipe. What recipe is best to use will depend on your tastes, but don't be afraid to play around and try a bunch of different ones. This approach is primarily used to help us from losing more money on our crops, but it can also be a ton of fun.

MINI FARMING

Chapter Summary

- What crops are most profitable for you will depend on local supply and demand.

- Head to your nearest farmers' market and conduct market research to see what is being sold, how much it is being sold for, and whether or not there is enough demand for you to earn a profit.

- Potatoes are a profitable crop because they are a staple of so many meals and can be used for a wide variety of recipes.

- Potatoes like to go into the ground after the last frost in the early spring when the ground is around 50F.

- Since potatoes grow under the soil, make sure to use a loose soil, or they will have a stunted growth.

- Potatoes like to be planted about a foot apart from each other and then covered with soil. As potatoes grow, you need to push the soil up around the seedling. This is called hilling, and it prevents the sunlight from messing up the potato and ruining it.

- Potatoes can be harvested three weeks after the foliage begins to flower. This produces small potatoes. For full-sized potatoes, you should wait until the foliage has fallen over and died. Two weeks after the foliage dies, that's when you harvest.

- You need to be careful when harvesting potatoes as it can be easy to damage them in the process and reduce your profits.

- Harvest potatoes on a dry day and keep them for a few weeks in a cool location to allow the skin to harden properly.

- Tomatoes need at least 6 hours of sunlight each day, a pH level of 6.5, and 60 to 80 days to mature.

- Tomatoes should be kept on the vine until they have fully turned red, and they are firm when squeezed. Tomatoes that have fallen off can be kept in a paper bag in a cool area to allow them to finish ripening.

- Tomatoes need to be planted with about two feet between them. Use a trellis or a cage when planting to offer support to the plant.

MINI FARMING

- Tomatoes don't keep very long, and storing them in the refrigerator reduces their flavor.

- Cabbage is a leafy green that you could harvest several times during the growing season.

- Cabbage sucks up a lot of nutrients out of the soil, and it will starve other plants it is grown with.

- Add extra nitrogen to your soil for the biggest cabbages.

- Harvest cabbages when it is dry out, cutting away any yellow leaves, but keeping all the green ones.

- Cabbage, like tomatoes, need to be sold quickly; otherwise, they will go bad.

- Onions are a fantastic crop to grow for profit. They keep for a long time and are easy to grow.

- Make sure to water your onions on a regular basis, as onions going through a drought will look healthy even when they aren't.

- Don't hill the soil around an onion; the bulbs need to be exposed to the sun to grow properly.

- Among the most profitable of all crops are herbs. These small and easy to grow plants, net significant profits, and they benefit the most from being produced in a hydroponic system.

- Jams and salsas offer farmers a way of taking their vegetables that were going to go bad and creating a new product out of them. Selling jams and salsas can be very profitable, and they also ensure that we don't let any of our harvest go to waste.

In the next chapter, you will learn all about raising specialty livestock for profit. Cattle, chickens, goats, and even bees are just some of the many animals which can earn a high return on investment and be raised in mini-farming conditions. We'll discuss the needs of each and the expectations that are reasonable to have going into livestock mini-farming.

CHAPTER FOUR

RAISING SPECIALTY LIVESTOCK FOR PROFIT

So far, we have mostly talked about growing crops. The vast majority of those who are going to start a mini-farm will be sticking to vegetables and fruits. But this isn't always the case. Raising farm animals can be a deeply rewarding experience that also happens to be profitable, and so we would be remiss if we didn't take a look at how we can raise our own. In this chapter, we'll be looking at how to raise cattle, chickens, goats, and bees. While it should be clear that one of the creatures on that list is not like the others, that difference isn't reflected in how much income they can put in your pocket.

Raising Cattle

Cattle can bring a lot of money into your farm, but they are also among the most expensive types of livestock that you could raise. You can easily expect to spend up to $20,000 getting started in a venture of this kind. This is exactly the easiest thing to do when talking about mini-farming. Thankfully, it is possible to start a little smaller, but you need to be extremely careful and mindful of what you are doing if you expect it to earn a profit.

To begin, you are going to want to get your hands on some healthy cattle. Whether you want cattle for beef or cows for milk, you absolutely must first focus on ensuring that they are healthy. Don't purchase cattle without first inspecting them, as this is how you figure out what condition they are in. You want your cattle to be alert and interested when they meet you for the first time. Yet you don't want them to be wild, as this is a bad sign. Make sure that you look into the eyes of the cattle you are considering purchasing. See if there is anything leaking out, as this is a sign of sick cows. Take a moment and place your hand on the cattle and listen to them breathing. There shouldn't be any wheezing or coughing, and the breaths should come in regular intervals. Pay attention to how they move and make sure that they are full-bodied, as a thin cow isn't a healthy animal.

Next, you are going to need space to raise them. You want to make sure that they have an area that they can graze. But you don't want them to get out and run away, so you should be able to put up a four-foot fence around the grazing area. You also need it to be big enough to fit a shelter so they can get out of the rain or snow. Finally, there should also be enough space for them to hang out and relax, away from the section where they graze. That means a lot of space necessary to get started. But, once you have the space, you can continue to use it year after year. While you are considering their physical needs, also remember that you are going to need to be able to transport them. You'll want to obtain a trailer designed to haul cattle, and you may consider either renting or purchasing one, depending on how much you are expecting to use it.

New cattle are going to be quite stressed out, as cows aren't used to being taken for a drive. Try to offer them patience and understanding, talk to them in a quiet and calm voice as they leave the trailer. Don't rush them or yell at them, as this is likely to make them want to stay in the trailer and hide. New cattle should be kept in a smaller location to begin with, just long enough for you to check them over for signs of injury. By reducing the size of the location they are first kept in, you make it harder for them to escape. They are less likely to escape once they have calmed down. If you have a barn, let them stay in it for a day or two. Keep in mind that this quarantining doesn't account for disease. You should research to see if there are any cattle-borne diseases in the area, and, if so, you might need to quarantine your new cow for upwards of 100 days. Of course, if this is your first cow, then you don't need to worry about this yet.

While cows need space to graze, this doesn't replace their diet. You still need to provide them with dry feed, and you might be shocked at how much of the stuff they can eat. Cows eat a lot of food, so be prepared. The grass they graze on isn't actually to feed them, but to help them to digest their food and keep their bowels in working order. Along with the feed, make sure there is always fresh water for them to drink, and you might want to consider adding vitamins or minerals to the water to keep them as healthy as possible. There are also many feeds that have been fortified in this manner. If your feed is fortified, then don't worry about adding anything to the water.

You should brush your cattle on a daily basis. You don't need to go over every part of them, but rather just brush away anywhere that is particularly dirty. This isn't done quite so much with the intention of keeping them clean; it's more to do with keeping close to them so that you can spot any signs of illness early. If any of your cattle are sick, then you are going to want to check their temperature, heartbeat, and breathing rate to help you diagnose what is wrong. You should also pay attention to how much they eat, as cattle tend to eat less if they feel unwell.

That's all there is to it. You need to provide food and water for your cattle, make sure that they aren't getting sick, and take them to the vet when they are. But beyond this, it is just a matter of time until they are ready to be sold. Or, if you have the stomach for it, you can also butcher your cattle yourself to sell the meat. But this process is much more involved, and many of us simply don't have the constitution for it. Selling fully grown cattle can earn you a tidy profit, so there is no need to worry about getting your hands dirty anyway.

Raising Chickens

Raising chickens can be a bit of a hassle. If you've ever had to go chicken catching, then you know exactly what I am talking about! But despite this, they are one of the more easy and profitable animals to raise. You can keep them in your backyard without a fence even, and you can get eggs and meat from them. Chicken feces makes a great fertilizer, and the shells of eggs can be added to the compost pile to make a nutritional mixture for your crops. Chickens will also eat worms and other insects, so they can serve as a way of reducing the number of pests you have to deal with.

Before you purchase any chickens, you will want to build a coop. A proper coop has space for a feeder and container for water. It must also have a roosting area and at least one nest box. If you only have a couple of hens, you will only need one nest box. But you should have three nest boxes for every ten hens you have. Keep in mind that you are also going to need to be able to get into the coop, as this is how you check for and retrieve any eggs that have been laid. Make sure that you build your coop out of a solid material, as nothing is more horrifying than having to clean up a collapsed chicken coop. Keep in mind that the size of the coop is going to be determined not only by how many chickens you have but also what breed they are. Typically, you shouldn't have less than three square feet inside of a coop. Chickens will benefit from more space, so consider going larger but never consider going smaller.

But before you even worry about building a coop, make sure that it is legal for you to raise chickens. Some towns don't allow any chickens to be raised on some kinds of private property. Others set a limit on how many chickens you can have. Make sure that you know what you are allowed to raise before you start investing your time and money into building a coop that you can't use.

Chickens need to be fed daily, but they don't eat as much as cows. Chicken feed is also much cheaper than cattle feed, so you don't need to spend much money to keep them fed. Purchase a 50-pound bag of feed and use that to calculate how much you are going to need to invest on a monthly basis. If you only have a couple of chickens, then this could even last you the whole month.

But the more chickens you have, the quicker they're going to get through the bag.

While you can sell the chickens themselves for their meat, it tends to be more profitable to focus on selling eggs. Hens typically lay eggs in the spring and the summer. If you live in an area that has plenty of sunlight during the fall, you can expect them to continue laying eggs throughout this season too. Hens lay eggs so often that you should make it a habit to check for new eggs once in the morning and once before bed. Keep in mind that chickens are almost like dogs and so you'll want to have somebody coming over and checking on them during the day if you have to be away from home for a bit. Make sure you ask them to check for eggs and that you warn them about how much chicken manure there is inside the coop.

You should never purchase only a single chicken. These animals are very social, and they like to be kept with others of their kind. You shouldn't purchase less than three, and you are better off getting five or six if you are legally allowed to. Since the average chicken lays an egg every day and a half, you can expect to get roughly an egg a day. As chickens get older, they will start to produce less. Typically this happens after the second year of life, at which point you may want to consider selling the bird to the butcher and purchasing a younger bird to keep the egg production higher.

Chickens that are crammed together are more likely to cause and spread disease. Chickens also need to get exercise, so they should have enough space around the coop to get out and spread their wings and run around a bit. Be aware of the possibility of predators, and take steps to ensure they can't get in. While wild animals like foxes are particularly associated with chickens, don't forget that your dog or cat will also rip them to shreds if given half a chance.

Where cattle can easily run you a few thousand dollars for an initial investment, chickens are a much cheaper animal. Building your coop will be the most expensive part, and this can easily cost you $500 or more. But chickens typically don't sell for more than $50 and can often be purchased for as little as $5. While you should be cautious about chickens being sold for such a low price, it isn't necessarily a red flag. Chickens breed like crazy, and so they often end up being offered at low prices simply so the owner can move the stock.

To make money from your chickens, you should primarily be selling the fresh eggs. Three chickens produce about seven eggs a week. So there's no reason you can't sell a carton of eggs each week. If you only sell them for $3, you can make back a $600 investment in 100 weeks or less than two years. At the end of the second year, say you send the birds to the chopping block and purchase three new ones. Even if you paid $50 a bird, it would only take you 50 weeks to make back the investment, and you could make another $150. If you purchased birds at $5 each, then you would make that back in 5 weeks and have 99 weeks left to earn profit. Of course, they are going to take the winter month off from laying eggs, but you can see how chickens can quickly start to pay for themselves off their eggs alone.

Raising Goats

Goats might not be the first animal you think of when it comes to livestock for your mini-farm, but they can be a surprisingly profitable investment. Goats can be raised for meat, but to get the most money out of them, you should keep them for their milk. They produce ten months out of the year, and you get close to 100 liters of milk from them each month. Not only that, but studies have shown that goats bond with humans just as strongly as dogs do. This means you can have a profitable milk-machine and a new best friend. As with cattle, you must prepare your property for a goat prior to purchase.

The preparation of your property doesn't need to be quite as extreme as with cattle, but you are still going to need to make sure you have a fence to keep them from wandering around the neighborhood. Goats are a tasty prey for large cats and dogs, so the fence doubles as a way to keep them safe. You'll want to be able to divide up the inside of the fenced area so that there is a location from them to shelter, another for them to eat, an area for milking, and an area for babies if you decide that you want to breed goats. Out of these areas, the shelter is the most important. You could always milk the goats in the middle of the field, and you can always keep the food around the shelter. But without shelter to protect them from rain, snow, and other environmental factors, you will find yourself with goats that are sick a lot more often than you expected. The shelter should be packed with hay for bedding and kept comfortable and regularly cleaned. It helps to make it a more relaxing area for the goats, and they will be able to return here to avoid stress, which would otherwise lead to more health issues or even a reduction in the milk they produce.

You'll also want to purchase supplies before bringing goats home. You'll need containers to hold their food, a mineral feeder to ensure that they get enough nutrients, and a water trough or a large bucket. You may also want to get supplies for bathing them from time to time, a brush to keep their fur clean, and maybe even a collar and leash to walk them. It may seem silly to walk a goat, but they thrive on exercise as it helps to keep their body strong and healthy. Speaking of healthy, you are also going to want to take a few minutes and open up Google to see what plants are poisonous to goats. For example, azaleas, china berries, black cherry, Virginia creeper, and honeysuckle are but a few plants that will make a goat extremely sick. Get a list of poisonous plants and make sure that there are none within the area you've fenced off. Goats are like cattle in that they graze on plants constantly. They love chewing grass, leaves, and any greenery they can find. They'll happily munch away on poisonous plants without a second thought, so it is up to you to keep them safe from themselves.

The final thing you are going to want to obtain is a First Aid kit. This is useful for your cattle too, but goats are a little more energetic and prone to getting into accidents. Get bandages, clippers for trimming hooves, and a proper syringe for injections. It is also a smart idea to prepare yourself by looking at the warning signs that goats give off to let us know they're sick. Some signs are easy to spot like coughing, gunk leaking out of their eyes, or discoloration of the face. Other signs require you to watch their actions to see if they are grinding their teeth, avoiding meals, pushing their head into a wall, refusing to get up, or isolating themselves. Finally, pay attention to see if they are chewing their food properly, whether their feces has become runny, or if their udder is unusually hot. These are just some of the ways that goats signal to us that they need to see a vet. You can always have a vet visit your farm if need be, but you should also have a trailer to take them in yourself. To help out the vet, you should listen to the goat's heartbeat, take its temperature, and keep track of any physical signs such as discolored gums or problems with their feces. That will make it easier for the vet to quickly diagnose your goat so you can get treatment for the problem sooner.

While even the healthiest and highest quality goat can get sick, sickness is much less common when you purchase from good stock. To do that, there are a handful of useful questions that you should ask whoever you are planning to purchase from. The seller should have an answer for most of these questions. Not being able to answer one or two is alright, but if they can't answer any of them, then there is a problem, and you should avoid buying from them. Begin by seeing if their goats are registered, as this is a good sign of a trustworthy seller. Ask how often the goats are tested for disease and what vaccinations they've had. Ask if they've had any goats die from disease. If they have, this isn't necessarily a bad thing. Follow up and get the story of what happened from them. If they are willing to share the fact that a goat has died of disease, then this is actually a good sign of a trustworthy seller. A candid seller is always better than one that lies.

Next, you'll want to know more about how the goats were raised so that you can more easily match your mini-farm situation to their expectations. Ask them about what they've been feeding them, how much fiber they provide, and how much milk the goats have produced. Moving from the seller's farm to your farm will be a stressful experience for the goat, and so you can make it smoother by matching your feeding to what they're used to. Less stress means healthier goats.

If you are careful to keep your goats healthy, they can produce milk for up to two years, at which point you could sell them for their meat. If you decide to breed goats, then you will need to be more careful about milking. Pregnant goats should be left to dry up and stop producing; otherwise, it can risk their health. Breeding goats can be quite profitable, but if you are after goats for their milk, then you are better off avoiding breeding.

Raising Bees

You might not think of farming and bees in the same category, but there's no reason you can't add a few hives to a mini-farm. Bees don't take up very much space, yet they can be incredibly profitable. Before you even consider purchasing any, you should first check with the zoning laws in your local area to see if you're allowed to. As with chicken, some areas don't allow bees to be raised on certain properties.

If you can raise bees, then the first step is to dedicate a space for them. Picking a location for your bees is a little like selecting a location for a crop. Make sure that they can get plenty of sunlight, though afternoon shade is also necessary. This means you should watch a chosen location and track how many hours of sunlight and shade it gets. Next, you will want to make sure you can provide nearby fresh water. Bees need water to stay healthy, and so you'll want to dedicate some water for them. If you don't, then you might find them coming into the backyard to hang out in your pool or birdbath. That might prove deeply unsettling for guests, children, or pets, and so you are best served by keeping fresh water as close to the hive as possible. When we keep bees, the hives are built into wooden structures. The wooden structure isn't necessary for the bees themselves, but they provide protection from wind and rain, which could otherwise damage their home. Bees like to be left alone as much as possible, and so you'll want to place them away from any areas that see lots of people or animals come through. If you have the room, you should place your hives 50 feet away from anything else. If you don't have the space to keep them at that distance, consider planting hedges or building a fence so that people don't disturb them. That has the secondary effect of keeping your guests, children, and animals from worrying about their presence nearby. Finally, you should keep the hives pointed to the south and raised off the ground. This will give them better use of the light while also protecting them from the elements and possible predators.

With your location prepared, wait until spring to get the hives put in. Bees are purchased in frames, which are then slotted into the prepared location. These frames are filled with honeycombs and are easily pulled out to drain the honey and check to see if the queen is laying eggs. The cheapest and easiest way to get started with bees is to purchase some packaged bees along with a caged queen, but this can take a long time to get a healthy and full-sized colony going. If you are starting out, then a more expensive but easier way is to purchase a nuc, which is a young hive made up of two to five frames of honeycomb. A nuc also has a young queen who has only just begun to lay eggs, which means that they'll be producing quite a few offspring at this point. It's important that you purchase a nuc from a reputable breeder. The other option that you have is to buy a full colony, though this is jumping into the deep end if you are a beginner. I would recommend starting with a nuc because it will be large enough to be productive quickly. Purchasing packaged bees will take longer to become productive, and beginners may feel like they aren't achieving anything with this slow start. By beginning with a nuc, you have the room to grow it into a full colony, and so you can be present for each step along the way. Then, after you have raised a full colony, you can start to think about expanding and purchasing another established colony to add to your mini-farm.

In order to install the bees into your farm, you should follow the instructions provided by the seller. If your seller does not have guidelines for how to install them, then they are not a reputable seller and should be avoided. This is almost the bare minimum that you should be able to expect out of a seller, so avoid anyone that won't offer this advice. They should be able to tell you how to install them, how to use the necessary tools such as a smoker, and they should have advice on how to work with the bees in a manner that won't stress out the bees or damage the hive. You will want to have a beekeeper's outfit, including gloves and facemask, as well as a smoker.

With your bees newly arrived at your farm, the first step to taking care of them is to raise them. Even though the frames you purchased are covered in honeycomb, your bees are nearly homeless when they are first installed. They need to build and make their home, as all you have provided them with is a frame. It might seem like it has walls and a roof to you, but your bees will feel differently. They are going to go through and seal up any cracks and start storing food. They're going to be extra careful to ensure the queen is safe, secure, and comfortable. To do this, they are going to need lots of food for energy. This food comes in the form of nectar. You might think this means planting a ton of flowers, but we can make our own nectar-like concoction that the bees will love. Take a jar and fill it up to the halfway mark with sugar. Fill the second half up with water and mix it around. You should have a viscous sludge. Use a feeder lid and store the jar upside down. The mixture should be solid enough not to leak through the lid. Bees will be able to drink from the feeder to get a sugar high that helps them build up the colony. In the first few weeks, you can expect them to drink nearly a jar of the stuff a day. But by the time a month has passed, they shouldn't need any more homemade nectar as they'll be heading out from the hive to find flowers nearby and feed on them. You can assist them by growing flowers in the area, but they'll find some even without your help. When you notice that they are doing this themselves, remove the feeder. The honey they'll produce using homemade nectar is nowhere near as tasty as what they produce when they make their own. In fact, you shouldn't sell the honey they produce in this early stage as it will only leave customers with a poor opinion on the quality of your goods.

As the hive takes shape, you'll want to be involved and watchful. Take a look at the hive at least once a week, as this will let you see how it builds and forms. Once you have a solid understanding, you can slow down and inspect once every other week or so. Keep an eye out for problems such as excessive bee feces, ant infestations, or problems with the queen, such as a reduction in eggs laid. You will also want to check for varroa mites and diseases like foulbrood. In time, the bees will grow too large for their frames and require you to add in some more. If they grow beyond eight frames, then a second box will need to be filled. Begin expanding by using a second box to support the original colony; the second one can be turned into its own colony eventually. Before you expand, however, you should think about protecting your colony by using an entrance reducer. That's only a simple block of wood that can help to keep pests and natural enemies out of the hive. When a hive is smaller, they're less protected. As the hive grows, the bees will have a higher defensive capability, and they can handle themselves just fine. You should keep in mind that an entrance reducer will also reduce the amount of honey you get. So, when the honey is at its most productive, you are better off avoiding a reducer.

If you have started your bees in spring, you might be able to get honey during the summer, but the chances are you're going to have to wait until the following spring. The bees typically need some time to prepare the hive before they start producing much honey. Expect to begin collecting late spring, the year after purchase. A typical frame will provide about eight pounds of honey. You can purchase specialized extractors to collect this, but beginners should learn how to do this on their own before buying expensive gear. One method is to use a scraper to cut off the honey from the frame into a container below. Don't worry about the beeswax; just collect it all at the same time. Next, use some cheesecloth or a strainer to filter out the honey from the solid bits of wax. This is left to sit until all the bubbles rise through it to the surface. From then, you can start to bottle and prepare your honey for sale. You'll find that the eight pounds of honey per frame has fallen to about three or four pounds after you removed the wax and let it settle. It might seem like you lost a lot of potential profit there, but there are ways to use this wax for larger profits.

Speaking of profits, we turn now to making money with our mini-farms.

Chapter Summary

- Raising livestock requires a much steeper initial investment, but it can bring a major profit in the long run.

- Cattle are the most expensive of the livestock we've looked at. They are expensive, and they require shelter, a large field, and lots of feed and water.

- You should always make sure that your cattle are healthy before you purchase them. Make sure to ask lots of questions before purchasing, Reputable sellers won't mind you asking, and they'll have honest answers.

- New cattle are going to be stressed out, so give them lots of quiet and give them some time alone. If they are your first, then they only need a couple of days. If you already have cattle, you will want to isolate them for up to 100 days.

- Cows need grass to graze, but they still get through a lot of feed and fresh water every day.

- Chickens are cheap, but they still eat a lot. They'll need a coop that is big enough to give them enough space to stay healthy.

- You should always check with your local township to see if it's legal to keep chicken on your property.

- Never purchase a single chicken; they are social animals, and you shouldn't have less than three at a time.

- Goats are as friendly as dogs, and they produce lots of milk. They aren't as expensive as cattle, but they still need a fence, room to graze, and a shelter to keep out of the elements.

- There are a lot of plants that are poisonous to goats, so make sure that none of them are present within the area you've fenced off for them.

- Make sure to only purchase your goats from a reputable breeder who will answer your questions about their health.

- Bees might not be what springs to mind when you think of farming, but they can be an extremely profitable investment.

- Bees will need a location with shelter from the wind and sun during the morning, but that's shady in the afternoon. They require water nearby, and a home where they won't be bothered by foot traffic.

- For beginners, purchasing a nuc is the best way to go with your first hive. It will be productive earlier but isn't so big as to be overwhelming.

- Create a mixture of sugar and water to help your newly-purchased bees settle into their space. They'll go through nearly a jar of the stuff a day, but after three weeks, you should be able to stop providing it. The honey produced during this period will taste much worse than normal and shouldn't be sold to customers.

In the next chapter, you will learn how to make a profit from your mini-farm. Farming may sometimes be a relaxing and enjoyable experience, but the end goal is still to turn a profit. To do this, you need to learn how you sell livestock, vegetables, eggs, honey, or whatever else it is that you've decided to cultivate on your mini-farm.

CHAPTER FIVE

HOW TO PROFIT FROM MINI FARMING

The goal for most of us is to make money with our mini-farm. It may be enjoyable to plant or crops or tend our livestock, but if we don't turn a profit, then we can't afford to keep our farms going. Thankfully, there are many ways in which we can earn a profit from our livestock and our crops. In this chapter, we're going to see some of the many ways in which we can do exactly that. We'll look at how our cows, chickens, and goats can earn us money. We'll see how our crops are able to bring us a pretty penny, and even how our bees can earn their keep through honey and additional products. There are lots of ways to turn a profit with a mini-farm, and I hope that those we'll look at get your brain working; a little creativity can come up with thousands of interesting and unique ways of earning a dollar.

Profiting From Chickens

An investment in raising chickens takes a little start-up cash. After all, not only do we need to purchase the birds, but we also need to build them a coop. If you have built it soundly, then a single coop can last you several decades, with minimal repairs and upkeep. This is great because it allows you to make an initial investment that you can pay off quickly so that you can earn profits within a couple of years. As far as livestock goes, chickens are among the cheapest to get started. But they also don't earn a lot of money out of the gate, so you should consider them as a long term investment.

The most common way of earning money from your chickens is to sell the eggs they lay. The idea might seem silly when you go to the grocery store and see a few hundred cases of eggs from half a dozen brands. Yet there is still quite a bit of profit to be made through selling eggs. Why is this? The answer is surprisingly obvious when you hear it. Out of all the large scale farming operations, raising chickens is often the most disgusting and inhumane. These birds are housed too tightly to be healthy, and videos of their abuse have been leaked online from several different sources. These inhumane practices have affected people. Many have sworn off eggs and chicken products, but there are plenty who have looked for alternative sources that act in an ethical way. That's where you come in. If you followed the advice in the previous chapter, then you have created an ethical and humane chicken farm, and you can sell your organic eggs for $5.00 a dozen. With six chickens, you can sell five dozen eggs in a two-week period.

Furthermore, once the hens stop producing eggs, you can then sell them off as meat. Egg-laying chickens aren't going to sell for as much as birds grown for meat, but you can still expect to get a couple of dollars per pound. But if you decide to raise chickens for meat, then you can have a quick turn around, as it only takes about two months for a bird to be ready to hit the butchers. Depending on the quality of the bird, which will be determined by breed and health, you can make upwards of $6.00 a pound.

While you may think eggs and meat are the only things chickens are good for, you should keep in mind that they poop constantly. This may hardly strike you as a positive, but chicken manure is great for use in adding nutrients to the soil. You may want to keep your chicken manure for yourself to use in your fields, but chances are there's going to be a lot more than you can use yourself. With a little bit of forethought, you can package and sell bags of manure to local farmers or gardeners. This little bit of creativity means more money in your pocket as you literally turn poop into cash.

Profiting From Cattle

Out of all the livestock we've looked at, cattle are the most expensive to get going. They need more space, shelter, and food than chickens, goats, or bees. Because of this, it can be easy to lose money on your investment if you aren't careful to keep them healthy and in good shape. But if you are able to provide them with the necessary care, then you can earn money by selling their milk or products made with their milk. You can also raise them to sell as meat, or you can raise a strong bull for use as part of a breeding service. Plus, as with chickens, you can use their waste as fertilizer for your crops, or sell it to local farmers and gardeners.

As far as profits go, milk is the best one because it is repeatable. But it also takes the most work because you need to milk your cattle twice a day. The laws around whether or not you can sell that milk are going to be determined by where you live. Some areas put strict regulations around the sale of milk, and this can make it pointless for you to purchase milk cows in the first place. Other places have rules in place to allow for mini-farms to sell their milk, typically with a limit on how many milk-producing cows you can have before stricter regulations are required. With these small-scale licenses, it's very unlikely you'll be able to get your milk into grocery stores. Farmers' markets and locally owned organic food stores will be your target demographic in this case.

Now, there is one way in which you might be able to make a profit from milk cows even if you can't sell your milk. The trick is to process it and create daily products for sale. Homemade cheeses, yogurts, butter, and more are all possibilities. These products often still require some form of registration or license, but many can be sold locally at farmers' markets without any problem. This approach is a great way to earn money from your cattle as you can use family recipes to make unique products that don't have stiff competition the way milk does.

Selling your cattle as meat is another way of making decent money, but it costs a lot up-front. To make it worth your while, you need to be breeding your own cattle; otherwise, you would just be purchasing cattle to resell them afterward, and that is a recipe to lose money in the long run. You'll need to learn how to breed your cattle, how to tell they are ready to be sold, and how to ensure they are as healthy and tasty as can be. If you have the patience to go through the process of preparing cattle for sale as meat, then you can earn upwards of $6.00 a pound. That might be the same price as top-quality chicken, but there is quite a bit more weight to a cow than a chicken.

Finally, you can also offer bull services to local farmers and help them in breeding their cattle. A strong bull will make for strong calves, and this is something that every farmer desires. Yet not every farmer needs to keep a bull around, as many only need one when it comes time to breed. By purchasing or raising a strong bull, you can easily make over $100 a month by selling its services. If you are breeding your own cattle, then keeping a bull around can help you ensure that your cows are tended to when they are in heat. You might not notice they've entered, but the bull will, and he'll know exactly what to do. Out of all the ways of making money off cattle, this is the most profitable when you weigh costs to income.

Profiting From Goats

As with cows, goats produce lots of milk, and you can sell this milk for a decent price. You will still run into issues regarding the legality of it as determined by your state, but regulations are often much more lenient than with cow milk. Unfortunately, goat's milk has a unique taste, and many people don't enjoy it. The reduced demand makes it a specialty item, which means that you can expect to make $2 to $5 more per gallon when compared with cow's milk. Some people have issues with digesting cow's milk or dairy, and so goat's milk is one of the alternatives that they turn to. If you have any specialty coffee shops in your area, then you should try to sell goat's milk to them, as they use a lot of milk and are most likely to offer these alternatives to their customers. Soy and almond milk are always popular, but local, fresh goat's milk is hard to beat and can make for a powerful marketing tool for these businesses.

If you are having a hard time selling the milk as it is, consider making products with it. You can always use it in different dishes, but one of the best ways to profit from goat's milk is to make bars of soap. Goat's milk soap is an anti-allergen, and so it is highly valued by those in the beauty industry. You don't need a license to sell soap. You can take it down to local markets if you want, but the best money comes from selling online. You can create a shop on Etsy for free, and offer goat's milk products that customers can purchase to have shipped to them. This opens up your mini-farm from primarily making a profit from the local area, and it taps into the power and interconnected nature of our modern society.

Eventually, your goats will stop producing milk. When that happens, you can always sell them for meat. Like goat's milk, goat meat is a specialty product. Therefore, it can be harder to sell, even more so than their milk. But if you have healthy goats of a decent weight, then you can net upwards of $200 selling them to the butcher or at the market. If you are breeding goats, this can be a great way to make a lot of money. If you aren't, then you can use this to purchase new goats for milking.

Finally, with a little creativity, you can earn upwards of $200 a day off your goats. If you have enough of them, they can be hired to help tend to lawns. Goats chew everything they can get their teeth on, so some people have turned this into a business and rent out their goats to serve as a natural lawnmower. It sounds a little odd, but it can absolutely make you a lot of money.

Profiting From Bees

Bees produce a lot of honey, which you can collect, bottle, and sell. You may want to sell this to local businesses, but you can also sell it at your local market or even alongside the road if you set up a booth. There are much fewer laws limiting the sale of honey when compared to the sale of milk. You can expect to make close to $50 off a gallon of honey. But remember that the honey we collect from the comb is very waxy and needs to be properly strained. You sell the honey that strains from that, but then you are left with a bunch of wax. However, this needn't be wasted.

Beeswax, beyond being none of your business, can be used to create many profitable items. One of the most common uses for beeswax is lip balm. Like goat's milk soap, you can sell beeswax lip balm online and make money from all over the world. Another product that is often made is hand salves. Beeswax has also been used in moisturizers, creams, eye shadow, blush, hair pomades, and other beauty products. If you keep your products natural, then you can make even more money through this approach; people are willing to pay extra for the knowledge that they are using natural products rather than those filled with possibly harmful chemicals.

Another way you can make money from your bees is to sell the honeycomb itself. Sold as a delicacy, the comb is a delicious snack that can be combined with meat and cheeses for a truly mouth-watering flavor. You can probably find local restaurants that are interested in purchasing your honeycomb. It has become more popular with the public in recent years, and it's also easier to sell honeycomb directly to customers rather than businesses.

Finally, to approach this with creativity, did you know that you can rent your bees out to farmers? Bees help pollinate flowers and plants, and this can help farmers to increase the size of their harvest. There are many crops that need to be manually pollinated, but even those which automatically pollinate themselves can see a major increase in the size of their yield when they use bees to help out. This unusual way of earning money often doesn't bring in a fortune, but the bees will keep producing honey at the same rate, and so you don't lose out. That means it's pure profit.

Profiting From Crops

What crop you grow is going to largely determine how much money you make off it. This number then changes based on where you live and sell and what kind of local supply and demand is in place. We don't need to dwell on this since it's been discussed previously. Instead, let's look at the three areas that crops are most commonly sold.

The first is the farmer's market, as we've mentioned repeatedly. Some markets require you to rent a table, but some allow you to set up for free. You'll need to provide transportation for your crops, and you'll want to bring enough money to give change to customers. Simply lay out your produce and let people buy them as they desire.

A more profitable arrangement is to sell your crops to local grocery stores. This can be a hassle with larger chains. They do often purchase from local suppliers, but they tend to have arrangements with larger providers, as the demand is too much for most mini-farmers. You are better off trying to sell to local organic stores or specialty grocery stores. They have a smaller demand, but they also have a smaller supply. Just make sure you grow your crops organically. If you don't, they're unlikely to want anything to do with you.

Finally, it may sound funny, but often the most profitable way to earn money off the crops you grow through your mini-farm is to set up a roadside stand. There might be zoning laws that prevent this, but these are pretty rare, as they are only usually active in urban areas with large populations. If you live in a smaller town, you're almost guaranteed to be able to do this. Which is great because it can make a lot of money. There is one such roadside booth that operates just down the road from me. The vegetables are left in baskets, and there is a money box chained to the booth. Each price is clearly listed, and the whole operation functions on the honor system, so it runs even while the farmer is out working the fields or taking his family to church. Even though it's such a simple system, it makes a lot of money. People claim that he grows the best tomatoes in the state, and people come from all over to purchase.

Remember, too, that you can always make salsas, dips, or sauces out of your vegetables if they aren't selling fast enough. You can also bottle and can certain vegetables so as to keep them for a much longer time, though these don't sell anywhere near as well as fresh vegetables. With a little creativity, you can probably come up with some amazing recipes that not only taste great but sell like hotcakes.

MINI FARMING

Chapter Summary

- Chickens are best used to earn a profit from the eggs they produce, as organic eggs can be a hot ticket item.

- When your hens stop producing eggs, you can sell them for meat. You can also grow chickens to sell for meat if you have the space and inclination to.

- While cleaning out chicken poop can be annoying, you can also sell it as a nitrogen-rich manure to keep the local fields healthy. Or you can use it in your own fields.

- Cattle are great for producing lots of milk that can earn a tidy profit, but there are also lots of regulations around the sale of milk that you should be aware of.

- If you can't sell the milk from your cows directly, consider using it to create dairy products like cheese and butter and then selling these.

- Cattle can earn up to $6 a pound when sold for meat, and you can even rent out bulls to help other farmers breed their cows.

- Goats produce a lot of milk as well, but it is a specialty item that sells for more, though it has a lower demand.

- Goat's milk can be used in a number of beauty products such as soaps, and these can then be sold online rather than just locally.

- Goats can also be sold off for meat; this is best done when they've stopped producing milk.

- You can even rent your goats out as all-natural lawnmowers to help weed fields or lawns.

- Bees produce lots of honey. This can be sold for a good price.

- They also produce a lot of wax, and this can be sold for use in beauty products, or you can make the beauty products yourself and sell them online.

- Honeycomb can also be sold as a delicious and natural snack.

- Some people even rent their bees out to local farmers to help them pollinate their fields for a bigger harvest.

- You can sell your crops at the local farmers' market.

- Local grocery stores may also purchase your crops, though they are more likely to do so from larger farms that can meet their stiff demand.

- A small-scale but profitable way to sell your produce is to simply set up a roadside booth and sell them directly to consumers.

- You can also take advantage of canning and jarring to preserve your vegetables before they go bad, or you can mix them up into salsa and sauces for sale at the farmers' market.

In the next chapter, you will learn how to prevent pests from infesting your crops and ruining your livelihood. These annoyances can make your life a nightmare, but we are able to manage them by practicing proper maintenance techniques to ensure we are growing healthy crops and animals. More than anything else, proper maintenance leads to better profits.

CHAPTER SIX

PEST PREVENTION AND MAINTENANCE CONTROL

With our mini-farms, nothing could be more devastating than losing a crop to disease or pests. These annoying problems can be easy to treat when caught early, but if they are left untended, they can quickly wipe out your entire operation. In this chapter, we'll consider the ways that we can maintain the health of our mini-farms so that this never happens to us.

Maintaining Your Crops

For the most part, you aren't going to need to do much to maintain your animals. The biggest issues that you'll have with them are going to require the help of a vet, and so you will have much more direct and actionable information to work from when you run into issues. But your crops are entirely dependent upon you. This means that you need to know how to tend to them properly and keep them in good health.

To begin with, you want to make sure that you aren't overwatering them. Too much water promotes the development of root rot, and this is one of the deadliest diseases. The problem with root rot is that it begins under the soil and so it can be hard to spot it until it's too late. As it spreads, it moves into the lower leaves, and you can possibly catch and stop it then, but a slight discoloration and odd feeling aren't easy to notice if you don't have a good maintenance routine. To begin with, avoid overwatering your crops. Always check the soil with a finger to ensure that it is dry. With most crops, you are better off erring on the side of drought rather than drowning.

But to prevent disease and pests, you need to get in and look at your crops daily. Being with your crops is the best way to get a feeling for how they are supposed to look, smell, and act. Yes, act. If they are falling over when they aren't supposed to, they are acting weird. If you notice holes in the leaves or discoloration around the edges, then there's something wrong. If they begin to smell wrong, this may be a sign of disease, but this particular sense is usually the least effective. I've only been able to catch disease in a crop once this way, but once is enough to earn a mention.

Spend time with your crops, and when you do, you can promote further health. Spray them with a treatment of neem oil every week. This is a natural product that does no harm to humans or pets, but it tastes disgusting to pests and helps to prevent infestation. You should also bring along a tissue and wipe the underside of the leaves as you move through the crop. If the tissue comes back with streaks of blood, then there are pests hanging out, trying to hide from your sight. The best way of dealing with pests when growing outside is to blast the plants with water, though aim it so that it goes away from the soil and not down into it. That will knock away a bunch and reduce the number of pests you need to kill. Next, you can release beneficial bugs like ladybugs. These bugs feed on the pests that feed on your crop. They will eventually head out to find their next meal once they clear away the problem.

As you are checking your crops daily, also remove any dead plant matter that has fallen off. While this can be added to the compost pile for later use, it is important to remove it at this point as it offers a place for disease and pests to grow. Removing it gets rid of the chance that it will invite disease into the field.

Maintaining Your Livestock

As mentioned, the biggest issue with livestock will be health issues. Always look in the eyes of your livestock to see if they are leaking any fluid. Feel the udders of your cows and goats to see if they're overly hot. Pay attention to how much they are eating and see if their poop is the right consistency. With bees, check the trays to see if the queen is still laying eggs, and to ensure that the larvae are surviving and growing properly. If you spot issues with any of these, then you will want to reach out to a vet or consult your local beekeepers' society.

But beyond health issues, there are ways that we can maintain our livestock to reduce the frequency of problems. For one, we can clean out the poop from their homes so that they aren't living in filth. Chickens, cows, goats, and bees are all negatively affected by living in their own dirt. It isn't much fun to have to shovel away animal poop, but it can be used to help keep your fields in healthy shape, so it isn't all bad.

Make sure that you are feeding your animals a healthy diet. If they aren't getting the nutrients they need, they'll get just as sick as your crops do. You should also make sure that they always have clean water. You might purchase a large water trough or container, but you shouldn't just fill it and forget it. It is essential that you check it daily to make sure that there are no feces or other contaminating materials present. Basically, if you wouldn't drink from it, then your livestock shouldn't.

You should also brush and maintain the physical appearance of your livestock. This touch is left out when you move up to larger farms, but it is very useful for raising the healthiest livestock possible. Brush off dirt and grime from them. Not only will this improve their appearance, but it will keep them cleaner and give you a chance to get in close and really observe the way they are acting and how they look. By taking the time to maintain their appearance, you also give them the equivalent of a doctor's check-up. Do this at least once a week, along with checking them daily, so that you can spot issues quickly.

If you spot an issue with your livestock, gather as much information about them as you can. Check their heartbeat, check their eyes, nose, and ears. Check their udders. Watch them eat and see if they show a lack of appetite. See how they interact with the other animals. All of this information will help your vet to diagnose the problem so that you can treat your livestock and get them back up to full health.

Chapter Summary

- While there are vets for your livestock, the only doctor your crops have is you.

- Overwatering your plants promotes the development of root rot, and this will kill them quickly. Only water when the soil is dry. Follow the recommended watering schedule for your particular crop.

- You should be checking your crops daily to get a sense of what is normal for them. That way, you can catch issues quickly because you notice when something stands out.

- Check your crops for signs of infestation.

- Apply neem oil to your crops once a week.

- If you have an issue with pests, then blast them off with a hose and introduce beneficial insects to the garden to feed on the pest.

- Remove dead plant matter from the fields to deny disease and pests a place to breed.

- You should be checking your livestock daily for signs of sickness, such as discharge from the eyes and ears.

- Bees should be checked to see if the queen is still producing eggs.

- Watch your animals as they eat to ensure there are no problems with their diet.

- Keep a close eye on your livestock's water. Contaminated water can spread disease.

- Taking care of your livestock's fur will keep them looking their best, but it also lets you get in and give them a once-over to see if there are any issues health-wise or any surprise injuries you hadn't seen.

FINAL WORDS

So there you have it, everything you need to start your mini-farm. Remember that farming techniques need to be adapted to fit the size of your farm, as following the techniques used for bigger farms is a recipe for losing money. To that end, let's take a brief look at the recommendations we've covered.

In chapter one, we looked at why you would want to start a mini-farm in the first place. If you've read this far, then I'm sure you already plan to start one, and so a recap of this chapter would just be beating a dead horse.

In chapter two, we got our hands dirty by looking at the different approaches we can take to grow our crops. We looked at monocropping and saw that it was a terrible option unless done in raised beds. We also saw that raised beds are generally the best approach we have to mini-farming and so I highly recommended you use them in your mini-farm. If you stick with growing in the ground, you know from our discussion that crop rotation is an absolute must. You also know that you can maximize your space by either using mixed cropping or intercropping. Of course, these assume that you have access to the outdoors, and not everyone does. For those without much outdoor space, we looked at how hydroponics can be used to start a mini-farm indoors. Chapter three looked at profitable vegetables that we can grow, such as potatoes, tomatoes, cabbages, onions, and herbs.

Chapter four saw us move from discussing crops to discussing livestock. Whether it is cattle, chickens, goats, or bees, these animals can make us a lot of money through the various products they produce. To get a sense of how we can profit from them, we spent chapter five looking at the products or services that we can offer. Finally, chapter six saw us look at pest prevention and maintenance with the goal of keeping our mini-farm healthy and productive.

You have all the information you need to start planning and making your mini-farm dream into a reality. But I want to leave you with one last thought before you leave.

Just because we are talking about mini-farms, you shouldn't think that these methods can't apply to larger farms. When starting out, it is best to begin with a mini-farm because it will keep your costs down and allow you to turn a profit much quicker. As your farm grows, you shouldn't feel compelled to stay small. If you are lucky and demonstrate that you care about your farm, your crops, and your livestock, then you can grow your mini-farm into the next major farming business. Just remember to keep to the organic and ethical guidelines that we discussed. It might be more profitable, for example, to stuff chickens together tightly. But, not only would that be unethical, anyone doing it would find a reduced quality in the product and, eventually, they'd lose customers. By staying ethical and organic, you ensure that your farm will continue for years to come.

Now get out there and start growing!

www.ingramcontent.com/pod-product-compliance
Lightning Source LLC
Chambersburg PA
CBHW050324120526
44592CB00014B/2042